CULTURE SMART!
BRITAIN

Paul Norbury

·K·U·P·E·R·A·R·D·

ISBN 978 1 85733 715 0
This book is also available as an e-book: eISBN 978 1 85733 716 7

British Library Cataloguing in Publication Data
A CIP catalogue entry for this book is available
from the British Library

First published in Great Britain
by Kuperard, an imprint of Bravo Ltd
59 Hutton Grove, London N12 8DS
Tel: +44 (0) 20 8446 2440   Fax: +44 (0) 20 8446 2441
www.culturesmart.co.uk
Inquiries: sales@kuperard.co.uk

Series Editor Geoffrey Chesler
Design Bobby Birchall

Printed in Malaysia

About the Author

PAUL NORBURY is a publisher, editor, and author who has written on international business practice and procedure, with particular reference to Japan and East Asia. He has specialized in publishing books on intercultural communications. Whereas previously he has focused on explaining Asian culture to Westerners (he is the author of the best-selling guide *Culture Smart! Japan*), in this book he draws on his experience as a mediator and interpreter to introduce his native Britain to visitors from abroad.

contents

contents

Map of Britain

introduction

In recent years Britain has experienced unimagined and accelerated change—from a population explosion due principally to EU immigration, with consequent strains on housing, welfare, education, and jobs, to a new political settlement based on coalition government, and the devolution of greater powers to the Scottish parliament in Edinburgh following the "No" vote to independence at the 2014 Scottish referendum—an event that generated enormous passion and attracted the highest turnout of voters in modern history.

There is constant speculation in the media about the shape of the future—including Britain's membership of the EU, the impact of what is now a multicultural society, and the consequences of the 2015 general election. However, what can be said with certainty is that Britain, as ever, will "manage" the change. It will "make do," "muddle through," somehow accommodate and absorb what it has to in order to secure the future and keep its traditions and core values intact.

The peculiar character of the British people has always intrigued visitors, who have described them as "enigmatic," "idiosyncratic," "eccentric," "reserved," and "quaint"—all of which contain a certain amount of truth. Britain has a reputation abroad for being insular and "different," sometimes annoyingly so. Equally, for the British there continues to be pride in the past and a kind of nostalgia for earlier times—epitomized in the highly praised opening ceremony of the London Olympics of 2012, and the very high ratings that period drama on television achieves.

As a family of nations, the British are inventive, reflective, good humored, funny, focused, and tenacious—qualities that have led to remarkable outcomes, such as the largest empire in history, a monarchy that has lasted more than a thousand years, and a parliamentary democracy that has been the template for the rest of the world.

Britain has produced some of the world's greatest literature, gave rise to the Industrial Revolution, was the source of most of the world's major sports, and has invented countless items of technology that have advanced the quality of life. It has won more Nobel Prizes than the countries of the rest of Europe combined, and has done more than any other nation to unite the world—first through its great trading empire, and then through the legacy of the English language. Its role and influence today has changed, perhaps declined. Yet Britain remains the world's sixth largest economy, and its entrepreneurial and highly creative culture continues to attract and fascinate visitors.

Culture Smart! Britain aims to help you gain that much more from your stay in these islands through a greater understanding of the quirks, customs, values, and changing ways of British life.

Key Facts

Official Name	The United Kingdom of Great Britain and Northern Ireland	Member of NATO, EU, G7, G8, OECD, UN Security Council
Capital Cities	London, the EU's largest city (pop. 8.6 million)	Other capitals: Edinburgh, Cardiff, Belfast
Other Main Cities	*England:* Birmingham, Manchester, Liverpool *Scotland:* Glasgow, Aberdeen *Wales:* Swansea, Wrexham, Newport *Northern Ireland:* Londonderry	
Area	Total area approx. 93,832 sq. miles (243,025 sq. km) *England:* 50,318 sq. miles (130,324 sq. km) *Scotland:* 30,297 sq. miles (78,469 sq. km) *Wales:* 8,021 sq. miles (20,774 sq. km) *N. Ireland:* 5,196 sq. miles (13,458 sq. km)	
Climate	Temperate	London temps. range from 36–43°F (2-6°C) in January to 55–90° F (13-32°C) in July.
Population	64.1 million (2013). Approx. breakdown: *England* 53.01 million; *Scotland* 5.29 million; *Wales* 3.06 million; *N. Ireland* 1.81 million	White: 86% Minority ethnic groups: 9.9% Principal ethnic groups: Indian, Pakistani, Black Caribbean, Black African
Family Makeup	Average members per household: 2.3	Pop. under 15: 15% Pop. over 65: 16%
Religion	Church of England, Churches of Wales and Scotland (Protestant), Roman Catholic	Principal minority religions: Judaism, Hinduism, Islam, Sikhism
Language	English	English and Welsh in Wales, Scottish Gaelic, Cornish

Government	Constitutional monarchy. No written constitution: the relationship between state and people is based on statute law, common law, and conventions. Parliament comprises two chambers, the House of Commons (elected) and House of Lords (unelected), and is the supreme authority of government and law-making.	
Currency	Pound Sterling	Symbol: £
Press	Daily "broadsheets:" *The Times, The Guardian, The Independent, The Daily Telegraph*. Also five national "tabloid" newspapers	The biggest daily online newspaper is *The Daily Mail*. Regional newspapers are published throughout the country.
Broadcasting	BBC TV has four main channels, 1, 2, 3, and 4, plus various other channels. ITV, the independent broadcaster, has many channels. The principal satellite channel is Sky; the principal cable channel is Virgin.	Radio is still dominated by the BBC, but there are many Independent broadcasters. Approx. 85% of households are connected to the Internet
Electricity	230 volts, 50 Hz	
Video/TV	PAL system	
Internet Domain	.uk	
Telephone	Britain's country code is 44.	Cell phone providers incl.: 3, Asda Mobile, EE, GiffGaff, O2, Orange, T-Mobile, Talkmobile, Tesco Mobile, Vodaphone
Time Zone	Greenwich Mean Time (GMT)	British Summer Time = GMT + 1 hr

chapter one

LAND & PEOPLE

WHAT IS "BRITAIN"?

First, a word about the different names used to
describe the country referred to variously as Britain,
Great Britain, the United Kingdom, the UK, and
England (the latter still being used by much of the
rest of the world, including the United States).
Correctly speaking, "Great Britain" comprises
England, Wales, and Scotland, together with all the
offshore islands, including the Isle of Wight, the
Isles of Scilly, the Hebrides, Orkney, and Shetlands.
The "United Kingdom" comprises Great Britain and
Northern Ireland. The Isle of Man in the Irish Sea,
and the Channel Islands, in the English Channel,
between Great Britain and France, are largely self-
governing, and are known as Crown Dependencies;
but they are not part of the UK.

The name "British Isles" is essentially a
geographical term, and describes all of the above

plus the whole of the island of Ireland, as well as the Isle of Man and the Channel Islands.

Britain is located on the westernmost edge of the continental shelf of Europe. It consists of two large and several hundred small islands that were separated from the European continent in about 6000 BCE. The mild maritime climate and gently undulating lowlands give the mainland an excellent agricultural base. The landscape becomes increasingly mountainous toward the north, rising to the Grampian Mountains in Scotland, the Pennines in northern England, and the Cambrian Mountains in Wales. The major rivers include the Thames in the south, the Severn in the west, and the Spey in Scotland.

CLIMATE

Britain's climate is often thought of as cool, wet, cloudy, and windswept. This generalization, however, fails to take account of the many regional variations in weather, or the microclimates that are found throughout the country. It is also a fact that, increasingly, for the UK at least, the worldwide phenomenon of climate change appears to be blurring the distinctions of the seasons, especially the autumn (fall)–winter–spring period. The British weather overall is controlled mainly by a series of depressions from the Atlantic that move across or pass near the British Isles on account of the prevailing southwesterly wind.

Talking About the Weather

Given the considerable variations in Britain's weather both regionally and historically, it is no surprise that there is a great deal of "weather talk" in the media, on

TV, and among the population: it is a constant topic of conversation and a routine part of social interchange. Freak weather events, such as the catastrophic flooding of parts of southern England in late 2013/early 2014, will occupy the headlines for days. Weather commentators will also insist on stating that it was the hottest, wettest, coldest "since records began," which actually only take us back to 1914 (under the control of the Meterological Office), although there are records for England going back to 1766, and even earlier if you include those of amateur meteorologists.

Historically, there have been many recorded "freak" conditions. For example, on January 21, 1661, five years before the Great Fire of London, Samuel Pepys recorded in his diary: "It is strange what weather we have had all this winter; no cold at all, but the ways are dusty, and the flyes fly up and down, and rose bushes are full of leaves . . ." On the other hand, on a few occasions, such as in 1683 and 1771, the River Thames has frozen over, providing an unexpected arena for skating and other amusements.

So, although Britain tends to be cloudy and overcast, the fact is that only about half the country has more than 30 inches (76 cm) of rain annually— except in recent years, as noted above, when freak flooding has overturned the precipitation tables. The wettest areas are Snowdonia, with about 200 inches (508 cm) of rain, and the Lake District, much loved by tourists, with 132 inches (335 cm). The wettest city is Glasgow with 170 rainy days (average) and the driest is Cambridge with only 107 wet days per year.

England itself generally enjoys the best weather overall, especially the southwestern part of the country, which benefits from its position in the path of the Gulf Stream (as do the Western Isles of Scotland). The coldest parts of Britain are the highlands of Scotland. On top of Ben Nevis, the highest peak, the mean temperature for the year is around the freezing point, while many north-facing gullies contain year-round snow. Air temperatures seldom rise above 90°F (32°C) or drop below 14°F (-10°C).

WHO ARE THE BRITISH?

Politically speaking, all the peoples of the United Kingdom of Great Britain and Northern Ireland, including the indigenous English, Scots, Irish, and Welsh, those from former colonies, and the many others who have made Britain their adopted country, are called "British." On the other hand, it is important to understand that the historic cultural traditions of the British, particularly the Celtic, Anglo-Saxon, Nordic, and Norman French cultures, remain at the center of the traditional "British way of life."

The centuries of conflict that were finally resolved in the Act of Union uniting the governments of England and Scotland in 1707 (the monarchies having united a hundred years earlier in 1603) generated a profound and, at times, fiercely defended sense of separate identity. This is, perhaps, best demonstrated in the national football and rugby teams for England, Scotland, Wales, and Northern Ireland. The matches between the four nations—especially those relating to the World Cup—are typically fought out with great passion, above all because they are a matter of national pride. But overall, most people (opinion polls and ballots prove this) would agree that there is far more to be gained by remaining united.

On the other hand, at the time of going to press, the great surge of Scottish nationalism that was prompted by the September 2014 referendum on independence shows no sign of abating. Although those in favor of retaining the Union won by a margin of 10 percent, the Scottish independence movement has continued to gain momentum since then and is likely to have a significant impact on the outcome of the British general elections in May 2015—not least in the balance of power at the Westminster Parliament.

Multicultural Britain
In addition to the indigenous cultures, Britain also has what could be called its "Empire" cultures—principally from the Indian subcontinent (5.5 percent), together with Africa and the Caribbean (2.9 percent).

According to the Office of National Statistics (ONS), the UK population is estimated to be 64.1 million (mid-2013). The 2011 census revealed that 14 percent of the population, or 8 million people, came from other ethnic backgrounds—numbers that have continued to grow. Today, according to the ONS, one in four children under ten are from mothers not born in the UK—some 12 percent of whom are from Poland. Britain, therefore, has the fastest-growing population in Europe, gaining a further 5 million since the 2001 census. These new communities are not evenly spread across the country, creating a very mixed pattern of integration and cohesion.

For example, about two-thirds of all Black ethnic groups live in London. In Leicester, Wolverhampton, and Birmingham, there are large numbers of Indians, and many Pakistanis and Bangladeshis live in Birmingham, Greater Manchester, and West Yorkshire, especially in Leeds and Bradford.

More than four-fifths of the total population of the United Kingdom live in England. The greatest concentrations of population are in London (8.6 million in 2015) and the Southeast, South and West Yorkshire, Greater Manchester and Merseyside, the West Midlands, and adjoining towns in the Northeast on the rivers Tyne (Newcastle), Wear (Durham and Sunderland), and Tees (Middlesbrough).

Following the passing of the Race Relations Act of 1976 (amended in 2000 and superseded in 2010 by the Equality Act), which brought about the establishment of the Commission for Racial Equality, now known as the Equality and Human Rights Commission, the government has actively promoted a policy affirming the multiracial nature of British society.

While such legislation is not universally welcome, it is generally accepted. The great cities are already largely multiracial (and multicultural) in character, and life is all the more colorful and vibrant for it; but traditional town or village life in Britain is still very far from this, and the advent of the UK Independence

Party (UKIP) reflects the view of a growing proportion of the population that Britain should now limit immigration and take back the power to do so by leaving the European Union.

Famous Names
Many regions and towns are associated with great English writers, artists, and musicians, such as Stratford-upon-Avon (William Shakespeare), the Lake District (William Wordsworth), Yorkshire (the Brontës), Stoke-on-Trent (Arnold Bennett), Dorset (Thomas Hardy), Worcestershire (Edward Elgar), and Liverpool (the Beatles).

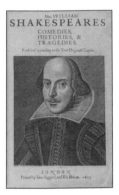

THE SOUNDS OF BRITAIN

The history of Britain has left a rich archaeology; but it has also left a remarkable "voiceprint" across the different regions of the country, with a great variety of accents, dialects, and vocabulary that can differ, even within the same region, from village to village and town to town. With more than 16,500 rural towns, villages, and hamlets in England, the majority having populations sometimes less than 500 or up to 3,000, many language variables came about.

If you link this to British history, and the story of how the island "mongrel race" evolved, it is hardly surprising. Even when Chaucer was writing his *Canterbury Tales* at the end of the fourteenth century, he was drawing on a Middle English vocabulary containing Celtic, classical Latin, vulgar Latin, medieval Latin, Saxon, Jutish, Northumbrian, Norman French, Central French, Danish, and Norwegian words! And since then, borrowed elements from the rest of the world have been added—from Hindi and Urdu to African-American rap.

Some visitors ask if there is a "correct" or "standard" way of speaking English. The answer is that for much of the twentieth century the BBC and other institutions tried to promote what came to be called "Received Pronunciation." Today, it is recognized that no such standard is necessary, and that regional accents all have their own innate value. Nowadays BBC listeners and viewers hear a variety of accents from all over the country, including what is known as the "flat vowel" sound (widely used throughout the north of Britain) in such words as "laughter"—pronounced "lafter," as in "patter," in the north and "laafter," as in "partner," in the south.

Accents and Attitudes

In his play *Pygmalion*, on which the musical *My Fair Lady* was based, Bernard Shaw wrote that, "It is impossible for an Englishman to open his mouth without making some other Englishman despise him." This neatly sums up the old situation, but while many would argue this is hardly true today, there are some who would continue to support Shaw's view!

HISTORICAL LANDMARKS

The British character has been shaped by the accident of geography and two thousand years of history. Successive invasions left their mark, the native peoples jostled for power, and collectively the British burst beyond the confines of their borders on to the world scene. At the end of this section is a list of significant dates in British history, which provides a useful point of reference. First, however, we look at the early centuries in which the foundations for the culture and way of life of today's Britain were laid.

In 55 and 54 BCE Julius Caesar sent expeditions to reconnoiter Britain for potential resources and settlement. Nearly a hundred years later, in 43 CE, the Emperor Claudius duly set about the conquest of Britain, which was followed by some 350 years of Roman rule over an evolving Romano-Celtic society. By the beginning of the fifth century, however, the Roman Empire was in serious decline, resulting in the virtual collapse of many of its outposts, including Britain. The remnants of the Roman army withdrew in c. 409 CE.

With *Pax Romana* no longer maintaining law and order, Celtic Britain was soon at the mercy of marauding German tribes—the Jutes (Hengist and Horsa), the Saxons, and the Angles. The Roman-style civil governments, or *civitates*, that were left continued to beg Rome, in vain, for help against the invaders. Eventually, England was overrun and became a predominantly Anglo-Saxon society, with the indigenous Celtic peoples pushed to the extremities—principally to Cornwall, Wales, Scotland, and, of course, the island of Ireland.

At the end of the eighth century, however, a new wave of invasions traumatized the people. This time, it was the turn of the highly sophisticated Norsemen— Viking pirates from Denmark, Norway, and Sweden— to wreak havoc and destruction, at least initially, on towns and villages along vast areas of the British coast. The first of these devasting invasions was in 793, when the great abbey of Lindisfarne in Northumbria— famous as a center of learning—was sacked and destroyed. The greatest Viking invasion, involving hundreds of ships—the biggest fleet England had ever seen—was to follow some seventy years later. This resulted in the fall of York in 867.

Over time, the Viking authority in many parts of England was firmly established. The administration of these areas became subject to what was known as the Danelaw. Place-names ending in –by, as in Whitby, and –thorpe, as in Scunthorpe, bear witness to their Viking past.

Today, the archaeological and cultural history of York is centered on an outstanding enterprise known as The Jorvik Experience, in the Jorvik Viking Centre located beneath the old city, showing visitors the different archaeological time-zones, with moving models, sights, and smells.

The next major milestone was in 1066, when the last successful invasion of Britain took place. William, Duke of Normandy, defeated the English at the Battle of Hastings on the south coast of England

and became King William I, known as "William the Conqueror." The story of the battle is famously celebrated in the Bayeux tapestry, presumed to have been woven in Canterbury, and kept today in Bayeux, northern France.

Northern French became the language of the court and the ruling classes for the next three centuries and French legal, social, and institutional practice greatly influenced the English way of life. When Henry II, originally from Anjou in France, was king (1154–89), his "Angevin empire" stretched from the river Tweed, on the Scottish border, through much of France to the Pyrenees. However, by the end of the Middle Ages (late fifteenth century), almost all the English Crown's possessions in France, after alternating periods of expansion and contraction, were finally lost.

England and Wales were brought together administratively and legally in 1536–42 during the reign of Henry VIII (his family, the Tudors, had Welsh roots). After the death of Elizabeth I in 1603, James VI of Scotland (the house of Stuart) became James I of England, uniting the two monarchies. The political union of England and Scotland took place in 1707, during the reign of Queen Anne. "Great Britain" was now the entity we know today.

Britain's great overseas trading empire dates back to the reign of Elizabeth I (1558–1603) in the sixteenth century, with opportunistic acts of piracy against the enemy, Spain—famously undertaken by the privateer Francis Drake who was second-in-command of the British fleet fighting the Spanish Armada in 1588. During the eighteenth century it expanded at the expense of its European rivals, making Great Britain the world's unrivaled naval superpower in the nineteenth century. The parallel story of Britain's great social, technological, and cultural advances, which have effectively created the modern world, has been the subject of many books. What follows are some of the milestones in the general sweep of British history.

Some Key Dates

55 and 54 BCE Julius Caesar sends expeditions to England (landing at Pevensey, East Sussex).

43 CE Roman Conquest begins under Claudius with 40,000 troops.

61 Rebellion by the Iceni people under Boudicca (Boadicea). Paulinus crushes the revolt after overrunning London and St. Albans. (Boudicca commits suicide the following year.)

122–38 Hadrian's Wall built to keep out marauding Scots, running from the Solway to the Tyne (partly rebuilt 205–208).

314 British bishops attend the Council of Arles, a fact that provides evidence of an organized Church in Britain.

406–10 Britain loses its Roman forces.

449 Landing of Hengist and Horsa. Jutes, Saxons, and Angles land in Britain and begin establishing the Anglo-Saxon kingdoms.

597 Roman prior St. Augustine is sent by the Pope to refound Christianity in Britain. He becomes first Archbishop of Canterbury.

664 Synod of Whitby chooses the Roman Catholic rather than the Celtic Church order.

789–95 First Viking raids (via Weymouth in southern England).

832–60 Scots and Picts merge under Kenneth Macalpin to form what is to become the Kingdom of Scotland.

835 Egbert of Wessex declared "King of the English."

851 Organized invasion attempt by 350 Danish ships. London and Canterbury sacked.

860s Danes also overrun East Anglia, Northumbria, and eastern Mercia.

899 Death of Alfred the Great, king of Wessex.

1066 William, Duke of Normandy, invades England, defeats Harold Godwinson near Hastings on October 14, and seizes the English throne.

1085–6 Compilation of Domesday Book, a survey of English landholdings ordered by William I.

1170 Thomas à Becket, Archbishop of Canterbury, is murdered by supporters of Henry II on 29 December.

1189 Richard I, "The Lion-Heart" (Coeur de Lion), is crowned, and sets out on the Third Crusade in 1191.

1215 King John is forced to sign Magna Carta at Runnymede. By protecting feudal rights from royal abuse, it set limits on royal power.

13th century First Oxford and Cambridge Colleges founded. Edward of Caernarvon (later Edward II) created Prince of Wales.

1314 Robert the Bruce defeats the English at the Battle of Bannockburn, ensuring the survival of a separate Scottish kingdom.

1337 Hundred Years War with France begins.

1348–9 Black Death (bubonic plague) wipes out a third of England's population.

1381 Peasants' Revolt in England.

1387(?)–94 Geoffrey Chaucer writes the *Canterbury Tales.*

1400–06 Owain Glyndwr (Owen Glendower) leads the last major Welsh revolt against English rule.

1411 St. Andrew's University founded (the first in Scotland).

1455–85 Wars of the Roses. Yorkists and Lancastrians fight for the English throne; the Lancastrians defeat Richard III at the Battle of Bosworth in 1485, and begin the Tudor dynasty with Henry VII.

1477 First book printed in England by William Caxton.

1534 Henry VIII formally breaks with Rome, founding the Church of England and setting in train the English Reformation.

1536–42 Acts of Union join England and Wales administratively and legally, and give the Welsh representation in Parliament.

1547–53 Protestantism becomes the official religion of England under Edward VI.

1553–58 Mary I ("Bloody Mary") supports the return of Catholicism and burns Protestant "heretics" at the stake.

1558 Loss of Calais, the last English possession in France.

1558–1603 Reign of the "Virgin Queen," Elizabeth I, and the Golden Age of the Tudors.

1588 Spurred on by Elizabeth I's famous rallying speech, "I know I have the body of a weak and feeble woman, but I have the heart and stomach of a king…," a smaller English fleet defeats the Spanish Armada.

1590(?)–1613 The plays of William Shakespeare are written.

1603 Union of the crowns of Scotland and England, when James VI of Scotland becomes James I of England.

1607 First successful English colony in Virginia starts three centuries of overseas expansion.

1610 Plantation of Ulster. James I settles Northern Ireland with English and Scottish Protestants.

1642–51 Civil War between King (Charles I) and Parliament.

1649 Execution of Charles I on January 30 at Whitehall.
The first and only regicide in British history approved by the people (Parliament).

1653–58 Britain becomes a republic, the "Commonwealth," ruled by the Puritan Oliver Cromwell as Lord Protector. He abolishes the monarchy, the House of Lords, and the Anglican Church.

1660 The monarchy is restored under Charles II (1660–85), hence the Restoration Period (the Anglican Church and the House of Lords also reinstated).

1662 Founding of the Royal Society (for the Promotion of Natural Knowledge).

1663 John Milton completes *Paradise Lost*.

1665 Great Plague—the last major epidemic of its kind in England.

1666 Great Fire of London begins in a baker's shop in Pudding Lane and burns for three days.

1686 Isaac Newton sets out his laws of motion and the idea of universal gravitation.

1689 The so-called "Glorious Revolution." A bloodless coup against the last Stuart monarch, James II, it results in his expulsion and the coronation of William and Mary. Resisted by Scottish Highlanders and Catholic Irish.

1707 Acts of Union unite the English and Scottish Parliaments.

1721–42 Robert Walpole is first British Prime Minister.

1745–46 "Bonnie Prince Charlie" fails in his attempt to retake the British throne for the Stuarts.

1760–1840 The Industrial Revolution transforms Britain.

1761 Opening of the Bridgewater Canal from Worsley to Manchester and the River Mersey (42 miles; 67 km); start of the Canal (transport) Age.

1775–83 Under the reign of George III (1760–1811) American War of Independence leads to the loss of the Thirteen Colonies. The Empire continues to expand in Canada, India, and Australia.

1801 Act of Union comes into force, uniting Great Britain and Ireland, governed by a single Parliament.

1805 Battle of Trafalgar. Nelson defeats the French navy. From his flagship *Victory* before the battle he sends the famous message, "England expects every man to do his duty."

1815 Battle of Waterloo and final defeat of Napoleon Bonaparte.

1815–1914 A century of expansion of the British Empire.

1825 Opening of the Stockton and Darlington Railway, the world's first passenger railway.

1829 Catholic emancipation allows Catholics to hold office legally and be elected to Parliament.

1832 First Reform Act eliminates a lot of "rotten boroughs" and increases number of those entitled to vote by about 50 percent.

1833 Abolition of slavery in the British Empire (the British slave trade as such having been abolished in 1807).

1836–70 Charles Dickens writes his novels, starting with *Pickwick Papers*; his last complete novel was *Our Mutual Friend* (1864); in the year of his death, 1870, he had begun *Edwin Drood*.

1837–1901 Reign of Queen Victoria.

1846 Repeal of the Corn Laws. Shift of power from landowners to industrialists.

1859 Charles Darwin published *On the Origin of Species by Means of Natural Selection*.

1868 Founding of the Trades Union Congress (TUC).

1907 Henry Royce and C. S. Rolls build and sell their first Rolls-Royce automobile (the "Silver Ghost").

1910–36 The British Empire reaches its territorial zenith.

1914–18 World War I.

1918 Women receive the vote.

1919–21 Anglo-Irish war. The Anglo-Irish Treaty establishes the Irish Free State; Northern Ireland (the Six Counties) remains part of the United Kingdom.

1924 First Labour Government led by Ramsay Macdonald.

1926 General Strike arising from Coal Dispute.

1926 John Logie Baird gives the first practical demonstration of television.

1928 Alexander Fleming discovers penicillin.

1931 National Government coalition formed to face economic crisis.

1936 The Jarrow Crusade—the most famous of the hunger marches in the 1930s.

1939–45 World War II.

1943 The world's first electronic computer, "Colossus I," built; used for breaking enemy codes in World War II.

1947 Independence given to India and Pakistan; Britain begins to dismantle the Empire.

1948 Britain's National Health Service (NHS) begins, offering free medical care to the entire population.

1952 The reign of Elizabeth II begins.

1973 UK joins the EEC (European Economic Community), precursor to the European Union.

2012 London hosts the Games of the XXX Olympiad.

chapter two

SCOTLAND, WALES, & NORTHERN IRELAND

The visitor should be aware that in Scotland, Wales, and Northern Ireland, despite superficial similarities with their larger neighbor, England, there are fundamental differences in self-perception, sensibility, style, and culture. So when visiting these countries a degree of sensitivity combined with at least an awareness of their different histories and distinguishing national characteristics will always be appreciated and will surely contribute to a more rewarding experience.

INTRODUCING SCOTLAND

The Scottish Highlands and Islands contain some of the most spectacular scenery in the world. Britain's highest mountain, Ben Nevis (4,409 feet; 1,344 meters) is in the Grampians. Scotland accounts for approximately one-third of Britain's landmass, but contains only some 8 percent of the population (5.2 million)—a population that is gradually declining, which is a cause of some concern within Scotland. The chief cause is the demise of traditional industries, such as shipbuilding and fishing, and only limited investment in the new high-tech sector.

According to National Statistics Scotland, the population is 98 percent white, of which 88 percent is white Scottish. Various statistical data suggest that as many Scots live in North America as in Scotland.

Scotland's two largest cities are Edinburgh (the capital, population 495,000 in 2011) on the east coast, and Glasgow (599,000) on the west coast; the two other principal cities are Aberdeen and Dundee. The least densely populated areas of Scotland are to be found in the islands—the most populated of which are the Shetland Islands (23,000), the Orkney Islands (21,000), and Lewis and Harris (21,000). In all, of Scotland's total population some 104,000 people are islanders, showing an increase of 2 percent in recent years.

One of the most famous places in Scotland is Loch Ness, the largest body of fresh water in Britain, said to be home to a "monster" ("Nessie"), which has captivated the imagination of the world since the first "sighting" by John Mackay and his wife in May 1933. Loch Ness is a major tourist attraction, and its secrets will no doubt continue to engage the worlds of science, literature, and Hollywood for years to come. At the time of writing, no monster has been found.

The next most famous place is probably the eight-hundred-year-old Edinburgh Castle. There have been strategic buildings and royal residences on top of the striking volcanic Castle Rock since the eleventh century, when it was home to Margaret, wife of King Malcolm III. It was later used as a military garrison and prison. The sheer rock-face and vast scale dominate the Edinburgh skyline and can be seen from every direction as you approach the city. The Edinburgh Tattoo, held annually in August over a three-week period and featuring massed pipe bands, is the principal annual event to be held at the castle, concluding with a spectacular fireworks display, an event enjoyed by millions on TV across the globe.

THE PEOPLE

Scottish culture remains vibrant, colorful, and homogeneous, with quite distinct traditions. The Scots have a strikingly clear self-perception and a strong commitment to their own way of life, despite (or perhaps because of) periods of mass exodus in the course of their history (see "The Clearances," below).

For example, they were prominent in the colonization of the British Empire, providing manpower, skills, and expertise in the engineering and technology of the time that effectively built Britain and its Empire. Today some 22 million people in the United States claim Scottish descent.

This "Scottish dimension" of the former Empire was in no small measure due to a strong sense of survival, persistence, and resourcefulness, and a superior education system, particularly in engineering, the sciences, and law, which is maintained today. The "colonization" process is now essentially limited to Britain itself—witness the key offices of state in the former Blair and Brown governments, as well as the Cameron–Clegg coalition government that followed, together with a significant number of leaders in British industry, the arts, education, the sciences, and the media (not forgetting football managers in the English Premier league!) who have Scottish roots. Following the 2015 general election, it is widely expected that many Labour Party seats in Scotland will be won by Scottish Nationalists, including the former SNP leader Alex Salmond, thereby changing the balance of power at Westminster.

Scottish Enterprise

The radical, nineteenth-century Liberal politician Sir Charles Dilke, who even went as far as advocating union with the United States (in *Greater Britain*, 1868), observed: "In British settlements from Dunedin to Bombay, for every Englishman who has worked himself up to wealth from small beginnings, you find ten Scotchmen."

Some of Scotland's Great Names

In letters, the writer and poet Sir Walter Scott (1771–1832) is probably Scotland's leading literary figure (see the Scott Memorial in Edinburgh), followed by the poet Robert Burns (1756–96), who epitomized the national spirit and continues to do so. The annual Burns Night dinners and parties

throughout Britain and the English-speaking world, which celebrate the poet's birthday on January 25, are testimony to the Burns "magic." Other great Scottish men of letters include Dr. Samuel Johnson's friend and biographer James Boswell, the novelist Tobias Smollett, the philosophers David Hume and Adam Smith, and the Labour leader Keir Hardie. The first edition of the *Encyclopaedia Britannica* was published in Edinburgh (1768–71).

Other great names include the essayist and historian Thomas Carlyle and the writers James Barrie (*Peter Pan* and *The Admirable Crichton*), Robert Louis Stevenson (*Treasure Island*), and John Buchan (*The Thirty-Nine Steps*). The most recent addition to Scotland's list of writers is J. K. Rowling, author of the Harry Potter books.

Arts and literature continue to thrive today, and the Edinburgh Art Festival and the Edinburgh Festival itself (in August) has become a world-renowned venue for all aspects of the performing arts; the Fringe, comprising hundreds of separate (often small) productions, is like an entertainment kaleidoscope, covering the sublime to the ridiculous. Two other summer events, the Jazz and Folk festivals, are also highly regarded nationally and respected internationally.

HISTORICAL PERSPECTIVES

Scotland was never a country that lent itself to conquest, nor was it ever conquered in any permanent sense until "conquest" took place in a political sense as a result of the 1707 Act of Union with England and Wales. This merged the English and Scottish Parliaments into a single Parliament based at Westminster, thereby creating the new state of Great Britain, and with it the Union Flag, which was the result of combining the two national flags—the red cross of St. George and the blue diagonal cross of St. Andrew, also known as the Saltire. (Interestingly, following the union of the Scottish and English monarchies a hundred years earlier in 1603, the first "union" king, James I, used the title "King of Great Britain" to signify the union of the kingdoms by one monarch.)

But, for some Scots, the historical relationship with England has been, and continues to be (especially for the Scottish Nationalists), painful. The memory of some events have remained in the psyche. Most celebrated, perhaps, are the Battle at Stirling Bridge (1277), led by William Wallace (later executed in London), and the overwhelming defeat of the English by Robert the Bruce at the Battle of Bannockburn, near

Stirling (1314), which effectively put an end to the attempts of the English King Edward I from 1296 onward to annex Scotland and impose English rule. This resulted in Edward III's formal recognition in 1328 of Robert the Bruce as Robert I of Scotland.

The Scots supported the Parliamentarians (also known as the Roundheads, because of the shape of the helmets they wore) during the English Civil War (1642–6), only later to suffer occupation, albeit briefly, under Cromwell's Commonwealth because of Presbyterian–Royalist uprisings in 1648.

There were many more uprisings, in fact, following the Act of Union in 1707. The most famous of these was led by Charles Edward Stuart, "Bonnie Prince Charlie," who after some success was finally defeated in 1746 at Culloden, near Inverness, in the Scottish Highlands.

"The Clearances"

There is residual anger over the infamous "Clearances" of the Highlands following anti-Union rebellions in the early eighteenth century, when the Scottish clan system was destroyed by the victorious English. In the early nineteenth century a great many tenant farmers and their families were forcibly removed to make way for sheep farming on a major scale. There were further clearances in the late nineteenth century, when sheep farming itself in many areas was superseded by deer forests. These clearances contributed to the mass exodus of Scots to the New World, particularly to New England, Canada (especially Nova Scotia), Australia, and New Zealand, and other corners of the Empire.

It is not surprising, therefore, that Scotland has sustained a strong commitment to the rights of the working man and the trade union movement, especially in Glasgow and the Strathclyde region. However, many traditional Labour Party supporters are switching their support to the Scottish Nationalist Party (SNP), which wants independence from the UK.

The Independence Referendum

The SNP agenda was fully explored in the run-up to the September 2014 referendum on independence for Scotland. This resulted in 1,617,989 "Yes" votes and 2,001,926 "No" votes—giving the unionists a 10 percent majority—perhaps the fear of the unknown triumphing over dreams of full nationhood. The voter turnout was a record-breaking 84.59 percent, reflecting the electorate's passion and political engagement. The "Yes" campaign was led by Scotland's charismatic First Minister, the SNP's Alex Salmond. When the results were announced he resigned and was succeeded by Nicola Sturgeon.

By way of compromise, Westminster immediately granted greater powers to the Scottish Parliament, including tax-raising powers, with the promise of more devolution to follow. However, such a devolution would be based on a new settlement within England, including a new principle of only English MPs being allowed to vote for English laws.

The Church of Scotland

The Protestant reformer John Knox was largely responsible for the establishment of the Church of Scotland in 1560, which is Presbyterian in the way it is run—that is, by elders as opposed to bishops—and based on the teachings of John Calvin and a strict interpretation of the Bible. (Knox's *History of the Reformation in Scotland*, 1586, is considered one of the masterpieces of Scottish prose.) In Scotland, unlike England and Wales, there is a division of powers between Church and state. The Church of Scotland's supreme authority is the General Assembly, presided over by a Moderator chosen by the Assembly. The British monarch takes an oath to preserve the Church of Scotland immediately following her or his accession, and is represented in the Assembly either in person or by a Lord High Commissioner.

The Scottish Parliament and Executive

Elections for the first Scottish Parliament in almost three hundred years took place in 1999 and the new, highly controversial parliament building near the old royal palace of Holyrood, its design led by the Spanish architect Enric Miralles, opened for business in September 2004. The Parliament has the Scottish

Executive and the First Minister at its head, and 129 members (MSPs), of which the majority at the time of going to press are Scottish Nationalists (64); Labour has 38 SMPs and the Conservative Party 15. The expected outcome of the 2015 general election is that the Scottish Nationalist Party will gain a considerable number of additional seats. The Parliament is responsible for the day-to-day running of Scottish domestic affairs. It does not have a second, revising Chamber, like the House of Lords at Westminster.

The Scottish Parliament's responsibilities include health, education, local government, housing, economic development, civil and criminal law, transport, the environment, agriculture, fisheries and forestry, sport and the Arts. In these matters, it is able to amend or repeal existing Acts of the British Parliament and pass new legislation. It also has the power to adjust the basic rate of income tax by a maximum of three pence.

THE SCOTTISH ECONOMY

Scotland is world-renowned as a leader in the production of chemicals, which represents one of the country's biggest exports. In more recent times, it has also become a leader in the "call-center" business, currently employing some 90,000 people in over 400 contact centers—Scottish "voices" are deemed to be engaging, professional and, importantly, reassuring.

Also of note is Scotland's proven track record in digital media innovation and creative enterprise, which supports more than 60,000 jobs. The industry covers a broad spectrum of businesses, including computer gaming, animation, film, TV, music, architecture, design, and the arts.

There are some 2,000 energy-related companies in Scotland relating to oil, gas, wave, tidal, and wind.

Despite the severe trauma of the 2007–8 world financial crisis, Scotland can rightfully remain proud of its 300-year history in financial services. Today, Edinburgh is Europe's fourth largest financial center by equity assets, employing 95,000 people directly and 70,000 indirectly. (The four Scottish-based clearing banks issue their own banknotes; these are legal tender throughout Britain, but are sometimes regarded with suspicion by retailers in England.)

Thanks to fifty years of electronics manufacturing and an enviable academic record in research, Scotland is a world leader in the electronics field. Recently, the industry has reinvented itself as a successful producer of high-end electronic technologies.

Scotland is home to one of Europe's largest life science clusters. Pioneering scientific breakthroughs include the cloning of Dolly the sheep, the development of MRI scanners, and the discovery of the p53 cancer-suppressor gene. Much of this cutting-edge technology is located in "Silicon Glen," in the corridor between Glasgow and Edinburgh.

Whiskey/Whisky

In Britain, the spelling is "whisky." There are more than a hundred distilleries in Scotland, most of which are in the northeast, and in 2013–14 they produced exports to the value of £4.25 billion (US $6.6 billion). Malt whisky, in particular, which is distilled according to age-old methods and some folklore, is relished and celebrated by connoisseurs around the world. Writers approach their task of providing critiques about malts almost as a sacred duty, and provide evocative descriptions and annotations in carefully researched reference books. Indeed, more than anything, whisky *is* Scotland.

The distilleries on Speyside and Islay, and in the Highlands are particularly well known and enjoy a very high reputation (some of the most famous being Macallan, Linkwood, Cardhu, Glenfarcias, Strathisla, Mortlach, Glen Grant, Glenfiddich, Tamnavulin, The Glenlivet, Tamdhu, Dallas Dhu, and Glenmorangie on the Durnoch Firth). There are more than 100 classified single malts, divided into the five regions of Highlands, Lowlands, Islay, Campeltown, and Speyside. The blended whiskies are the most common worldwide, but malt whisky consumption is growing as drinkers discover the wide-ranging subtleties that exist. Has the water that goes into the making of the malt, for example, been filtered through peat or over granite? Is the shape of the still significant? Has the barley been home grown or imported? It's all in the "nose"!

Whisky wasn't always Scotland's top tipple. In the seventeenth and eighteenth centuries the favored drink was claret, shipped in from Bordeaux to Leith. Indeed,

Robert Burns himself testified to the vast quantities that were consumed in his song, "Gae bring tae me a point o'wine." The tax on wine put an end to its popularity, and gave the cue for the old illegal stills to go public (and legal) and develop the high value-added whisky industry that exists today.

Of Dallas Dhu distillery, established in 1899, the distinguished connoisseur and writer Wallace Milroy offers the following information in his *Malt Whisky*: "Nose: Delicate touch of peat. Taste: Full-bodied, lingering flavor and smooth aftertaste . . . . The entire distillery is now run by Historic Buildings and Monuments and is an excellent place to visit. An after-dinner dram available from the distillery and the independent bottlers. Also, the Scotch Whisky Heritage Centre in Edinburgh provides a comprehensive introduction to the whisky industry and its 'water of life.'"

THE BAGPIPES

Although known to the Egyptians and Romans millennia ago, there is no doubt that today the "sound" of Scotland is the bagpipes, and has been so for centuries. The earliest piping competitions took place at the annual Falkirk Tryst in 1781, when a Highlander could be penalized for wearing the kilt or playing the "warlike" instrument, as it was then considered.

There is no sound on earth so stirring and elemental as that of massed pipes. The band of the Queen's Own Cameron Highlanders and others can be heard daily at Edinburgh Castle during the Edinburgh Tattoo in August, and at other major public occasions such as Highland Gatherings (games), most famously the Cowal Highland Gathering (Cowal Games) held in Dunoon every August. The games invariably include pipe concerts and competitions. In the old days, most clan chiefs boasted a personal piper—a tradition that gave rise to legendary piping families, such as the MacCrimmons, the MacLeods, and the

MacArthurs. Towns, police departments, and Highland regiments have pipe bands—among the most famous is the Shotts and Dykehead Caledonia Pipe Band.

Hogmanay

This is the Scottish name for the last day of the year, and also for the oatmeal cakes traditionally given to the children as they went from house to house singing carols. Now it is more a media event, and is all to do with partying and having a good time—televised live from Edinburgh Castle's Great Hall by BBC Scotland as one of the nation's annual festivities.

CLANS AND TARTANS

Scottish life and culture used to be split between the Lowlands or Borders cities, towns, and villages, where intellectual, scientific, and literary life was nurtured, and the Highlands, where social life revolved around the clan system, *clann* in Gaelic meaning children or family.

Loyalty was paramount for survival since the clan chief was at once leader, protector, and dispenser of justice. (Still to be seen today are the gallow hills and beheading pits, which were common features of clan territories.) The ties of kinship created a strong and at times very powerful social unit. Clan feuds, popularized by Sir Walter Scott in his novel *Rob Roy*, were commonplace and frequently deadly. The Scottish monarchs tended to leave the Highlands well alone.

After the final crushing defeat of the Scots at the Battle of Culloden in 1746, sweeping changes to the Highland way of life were introduced with the Act of Proscription (1747), which outlawed the wearing of tartan in any form (including kilts) and the carrying of arms. In addition, heritable (clan) jurisdictions were abolished and even the bagpipes could not be played in public. In fact, anything to do with Highland life was deemed undesirable. The Clearances helped to sweep away the old Highland culture.

However, in 1782 the Act of Proscription was repealed, which led to the commercialization and standardization of tartans, with the first tartan pattern books becoming available shortly after. Historians note that George lV wore a tartan on his visit to Scotland in 1822, which gave rise to a nineteenth-century tartan boom, nurtured by Queen Victoria, who had a special fondness for the Highlands. Her personal servant (and in later life companion) John Brown was from Aberdeenshire.

Today, a tartan exists for every occasion, whether it be for everyday wear, hunting, or "dress" wear. Given the advances in the weaving and dyeing industry, it is not surprising that tartan links to the historic clans have become increasingly stretched, giving rise to the more than 2,500 tartans and variations now controlled by the official government Scottish Register of Tartans (www.tartanregister.gov.uk).

GOLF

Golf—widely recognized as one of the world's oldest, most sophisticated, and most prestigious sports—has come a long way since the ancient game of *gowff*, which involved whacking a stone with a stick. The earliest mention of golf as a game that we would recognize goes back to 1457, when its popularity was so great that it (along with "futeball") had to be prohibited on Sundays because it interfered with archery practice. In 1754 a society of golfers was formed at the ancient university city of St. Andrews. In 1834, under the patronage of William IV, this became the Royal and Ancient Golf Club of St. Andrews, and the ruling body of the game in Britain.

FOOD AND HOME

The Scots may be dour, cautious, and candid, but they are friendly people and are widely known for their warm and hospitable welcome to the visitor. It is also sometimes said that they are not given to as much laughter as the English; but to say so is to belie the fact that in recent years some of the best stand-up comedians who have made their name in England come from Scotland, including Ronnie Corbett, Billy Connolly, Frankie Boyle, Kevin Bridges, and Susan Calman.

Traditionally, the Scottish diet was dominated by oats. A typical main meal would be "tatties and herring," which is potatoes with herring in oatmeal. The popularity of oats lives on today in porridge, oatcakes, flapjacks, and such delicious sweetened dishes as Atholl brose and cranachan, both of which contain oatmeal, with various additions such as honey, cream, raspberries, and whisky or Drambuie.

The national dish, haggis, is traditionally enjoyed on Burns Night, "piped in" by a lone piper. It comes in various sizes and consists of chopped offal mixed with suet, oatmeal, onions, and herbs, and boiled in the stomach of a sheep, which for years gave the EU some headaches, resulting in an "approved" synthetic lining now used instead. The haggis is traditionally eaten with mashed potatoes and turnips, or may be presented in a variety of imaginative and delicious ways; there is even a vegetarian version. Other favorites include the richly fruited Dundee cake, shortbread, beef, venison, and several varieties of smoked fish—most recently Scottish smoked salmon has become a major industry supplying both domestic and international markets.

Choose Your Moment!
Visitors to Scotland should probably be aware of one old custom—if a bottle of whisky is opened for a guest it has to be entirely consumed before the household retires for the night—and thus should choose the time of their visit accordingly!

Home Life
The most distinguishing common features of Scotland's main cities are the late nineteenth-century tenement buildings, built by developers and entrepreneurs. With eight or more homes (apartments) to a block, they housed the workers who labored in the mills and factories, shops and

stores, docks and transport systems that produced the wealth of Victorian Britain.

The tenements were hardly commodious, but somehow the large families common at that time managed with one or two bedrooms (the second bedroom was usually more of a box-room), a front room (which doubled as another bedroom), a kitchen, and a bathroom. Heating was by open coal fires. A common garden area at the back was used for recreation and washing lines. One such home, at 145 Buccleuch Street, Glasgow, is open to the public. Housing one family continuously from 1911 to the 1960s, it is now a museum of tenement life. Once renovated and refurbished, tenements are today much sought after—especially by the younger generation.

If you were in one of the leading professions—a doctor, a lawyer, or a consulting engineer—in Edinburgh, which is also considered the "snob" capital of Scotland—your home would be in one of the spacious and splendid Georgian terraces on the west side of the city.

The Edinburgh social scene is predictably very closely knit, and the lighter, more refined Edinburgh accent stands out in contrast to the richer brogues of Glasgow and elsewhere. People from Aberdeen, to the northeast, are sometimes said to speak the purest English in Britain, on account of their traditional "clean" and "clear" pronunciation of English, albeit with a very defined and rolled "r."

Edinburgh may see itself as Scotland's center of excellence, but Glasgow is the heart of the country. A vast, sprawling city, capital of the Strathclyde region, with enormous contrasts in wealth and poverty, it has great character and panache, and an amazing array of subcultures. Some of the downtown dialects are almost

incomprehensible, even to other Scots. Glasgow boasts some of the finest specimens of Victorian and modern architecture, and has been recognized as the Garden City, the City of Culture, and the City of Architecture, which celebrated the enormous contributions its famous son, Charles Rennie Mackintosh (1868–1928) made to the place with his distinctive designs, especially his masterpiece, the Glasgow School of Art. Sadly, the school's iconic library—recognized as one of the finest examples of *art nouveau* in the world—suffered severe fire damage in May 2014. Fortunately none of the school's archives was lost.

Also, Glasgow *is* football (soccer), epitomized in two teams, Celtic and Rangers, the former being the Catholic and the latter the Protestant football team (never confuse the two!). Both teams teams battle for first place in the Scottish Premier Football Division.

EDUCATION

The Scottish education system has a number of distinctive features, including the structure and organization of schools, a separate system of examinations, and differences in the curriculum. Record numbers of students continue with vocational, further, or higher education; and, unlike England and Wales, Scotland offers a very supportive financial package to students going on to continue their studies, especially at university.

GAELIC

Scottish Gaelic is a Celtic language, akin to Irish. As a spoken language it is being actively supported by the Scottish Parliament (Pàrlamaid na h-Alba, in Gaelic), with currently some 60,000 speakers who are competent enough to use it as a first language. The Gaelic Language Act of 2005 seeks to "accord equal status" to English and Gaelic. Most of today's Gaelic speakers live in the Hebrides (where over 70 percent are Gaelic speakers) and Skye (about 60 percent), off Scotland's west coast. The main institution for Gaelic culture is the An Commun Gàidhealach, based in Inverness.

INTRODUCING WALES

In Welsh, it is known as *Cymru*, which roughly translates as "the country of friends." In English it is known simply as Wales—a land of chapels, valleys, and hill farming, and vast, empty, mountainous spaces. It is the land where there is a growing passion to speak the Welsh language and consequently where, uniquely in Britain, most official signs and notices are bilingual. Wales is also the land of the male voice choir—one of the signally beautiful things that emerged out of the dark and dangerous era of coal mining and the iron foundries—now, mercifully, long gone. Among the most famous contemporary choirs are the Morriston Orpheus, Cowbridge, Gwalia, and Bridgend. Welsh male voice choirs are also to be found in London, Oxford and elsewhere.

Not surprisingly, given the ethereal beauty of its geography and ever-changing climate, sitting as it does as Britain's front door to the prevailing weather systems of the Atlantic, Wales is also a source of inspiration to writers, musicians, artists, and craftspeople from around the world. All this is encapsulated in the annual Welsh cultural festival, the *Eisteddfod*, where lyrical poetry is sung to a harp accompaniment and male voice choirs go for gold.

On Arrival

Visitors to Wales will quickly become aware that they are in a "foreign" country: the Welsh language is spoken widely—although this is not so evident in

metropolitan Cardiff—and appears on all road signs, public notices, and official buildings. Don't try to pronounce Welsh: it is full of consonants, and requires assiduous study! Apart from some isolated areas where Welsh is the first language, everyone also speaks English and you will be warmly welcomed as a visitor. According to the 2011 census, the percentage of the population who can speak Welsh dropped from 21 percent in 2001 to 19 percent. Gwynedd is the only region where more than half the population speaks, reads, and writes Welsh. BBC Cymru Wales broadcasts in both English and Welsh.

Most road signs in Wales are bilingual, and Welsh is used equally with English in the Welsh Assembly. Since 2000 it has been taught as a first or second language to pupils throughout Wales; in addition, it is used as a first teaching language in a number of primary and secondary schools in Wales. Proposals to increase Welsh language teaching in Wales is an ongoing controversial subject. The Welsh language has a unique, undulating rhythm, which has transferred to the accent of the Welsh when speaking English.

You may find aspects of local life, traditionally informed by a strict chapel Methodism, very parochial, and the people not especially enthusiastic about the English. But that shouldn't deter you from enjoying the rich Celtic culture and its traditions that are there to be discovered.

GEOGRAPHY

The most famous of the Welsh highland areas is Snowdonia National Park in the north of the country, which spreads across some 825 square miles (2,137 sq. km), with Snowdon (*Yr Wyddfa*), its highest

peak, rising to 3,560 feet (1,085 m). But although the north is the most mountainous area, there are also delightful upland areas of central Wales. The Severn, at 210 miles (338 km), is the longest river in Britain. The Brecon Beacons are the center of another National Park of about 500 square miles (l,300 sq. km). The Welsh mountains are important sources of water for Wales, and for major English cities such as Liverpool and Birmingham.

SOME HISTORY

Long before the Romans left Britain, Wales was an autonomous Celtic stronghold ruled by sovereign princes. But by the eleventh century, the emerging Anglo-Norman kingdom of England found it increasingly difficult to maintain law and order along its borders resulting from the rivalry that was rife among the Welsh princes. William the Conqueror had himself attempted to find a solution (without much success) to what came to be known as the "Welsh problem," and in the second half of the twelfth century Henry II set up a system of "divide and rule" schemes involving small areas of jurisdiction whereby his famous, and often ruthless, Anglo-Norman Marcher barons held power in key places such as Chepstow, Brecon, and  Monmouth. (The so-called Marcher barons were appointed to supervise the Marches, the boundary areas of England with Wales, and also with Scotland.)

Matters came to a head in December 1282 when Edward I, through his Marcher barons, brought

Wales under English rule by defeating the last Welsh prince, Llywelyn ap Gruffydd, at the battle of Orewin Bridge in mid-Wales. This signaled the end of any hope of an independent country. Edward consolidated his position by building a series of magnificent and impregnable castles in strategic places across Wales. The sheer scale of the building project was breathtaking, greater than anything that had taken place in Europe before, or has taken place since. It was supervised by a master builder known as Master James of St.-George, and these castles,

including Aberystwyth, Harlech, Caernarvon, Conway, and Flint, are some of the finest historic monuments in Britain today. As one historian has since observed, nothing like this had happened in Britain since the building of Hadrian's Wall (begun in 122 CE under the Emperor Hadrian).

To further make his point about who was in charge, Edward I's son, later Edward II, was born in Caernarvon Castle in 1284 and declared the first English Prince of Wales. The eldest son of the reigning monarch still traditionally bears this title; Prince Charles was made Prince of Wales in 1969.

By the turn of the fifteenth century, Welsh resentment over English laws and administration, together with widespread poverty and economic hardship, brought the nationalist leader Owain Glyndwr (Owen Glendower) into open confrontation with King Henry IV. After some initial success against the English, Glyndwr was defeated by Henry and the

Prince of Wales at the Battle of Shrewsbury in 1403. The Welsh may have been defeated, but before the century was out, blood ties linked them inextricably to the English monarchy.

With the accession of Henry VII in 1485, the Tudor dynasty came into being, bringing with it important Welsh ancestry. As a result, under Henry VIII, two key Acts of Union in 1536 and 1542 united England and Wales administratively, politically, and legally. This has remained the case until the present day; hence you will see references to the laws "governing England and Wales," while Scotland and Northern Ireland have their own legislatures and legal systems.

A referendum was held in Wales in 1997, as part of the then Labour government's policy of devolution, to decide whether Wales should have an independent Assembly with some control over Welsh affairs (the National Assembly for Wales). The referendum attracted few voters (about a third of the electorate), with those in favor coming barely ahead of those who rejected the idea. Nevertheless, it may be seen in years to come as a turning point in Welsh history. The Assembly is responsible for education, health, business, culture, and sport. Westminster continues to control foreign affairs, defense, taxation, overall economic policy, crime, justice, prisons, social security, and broadcasting.

COAL AND IRON
In the eighteenth and nineteenth centuries, the Industrial Revolution had a major impact in south Wales, where the iron and steel factories and the coal mines were concentrated. The capital, Cardiff, grew in the nineteenth century as a coal exporting port, and

Swansea and Newport also depended for their prosperity on the surrounding industries as well as their position as ports in the Bristol Channel. Among the most famous steel towns were Merthyr Tydfil and Ebbw Vale. Over time, of course, all the valleys where coal was accessible attracted settlers. The coal was transported to the ports by railways and canals—most famously, the Monmouthshire canal to Newport, which opened in 1791.

THE WELSH ECONOMY

In 2006, the Welsh Development Agency was abolished and its remit transferred to the Welsh Assembly. This was viewed by some as a controversial decision because it removed the high international profile the WDA once had—attracting considerable levels of inward investment and the many thousands of jobs that followed. The historic landmark was the arrival of Sony and its Technology Center in 1992, based at Bridgend in South Wales. It is the only center outside Japan to produce high definition camera units. Today there are several significant areas of high-end manufacturing in Wales.

Aereospace and Defense

Wales is home to 160 companies employing 23,000 people, with an annual turnover of around £5 billion. Some of the world's biggest aerospace and defense companies have bases in Wales, including Airbus, GE Aviation, BAE Systems, and Nordam. In addition,

British Airways has three Maintenance and Repair and Operations (MRO) facilities in south Wales.

Wales undertakes around 25 percent of the UK's aerospace MRO activity. The Airbus wing manufacturing center in Broughton is the biggest aerospace manufacturing operation in the UK.

Automotive

Wales is home to 185 companies employing over 16,000 people, with a turnover of £3 billion annually. A significant number of "Tier 1" suppliers, including Ford and Toyota—serviced by an established, diverse supply chain—are based in Wales.

Wales has particular expertise in alternative fuels (including hydrogen research and technology) and is a leading UK region for developing a low-carbon infrastructure for vehicles in collaboration with Welsh academic centers of excellence,

Opto-electronics

The Welsh Opto-electronics Skills Survey (2013) identifies 85 opto-electronic businesses in Wales, employing some 5,000 people, with a turnover of £1 billion.

Other key technologies are represented in Wales, including communications, modern optics, electro-optics, instrumentation, sensors, lasers, fiber optics, thin film coating, conventional optics and optical design, solar cells (photovoltaics), optical storage, displays, imaging, photonic materials, and holography.

THE PEOPLE AND THE LANGUAGE

The population of Wales is just over three million, with more than half living in the industrialized south.

Cardiff is the largest city (population 350,000), followed by Swansea (240,000).

In common with other Celtic cultures, such as those found in Scotland and Ireland, the Welsh love theater, poetry, oratory, debate, and storytelling, and, as already noted, they love to sing—talents and preoccupations that are all represented among the great names of past and present.

Some 20 percent of the population are Welsh speakers, with Welsh being the first language spoken in the rural north and west of the country.

Some Famous Names

Twentieth-century politicians include David Lloyd George, the Liberal Prime Minister during the First World War, Aneurin Bevan, who inaugurated the British National Health Service after the Second World War, and Neil Kinnock, who led the Labour Party in the 1980s. The names of the poet Dylan Thomas, the singers Tom Jones, Shirley Bassey, Bryn Terfel, mezzo-soprano Catherine Jenkins, and the film stars Richard Burton, Anthony Hopkins, and Catherine Zeta Jones are world famous.

Welsh Crafts

Craftwork is a living tradition in Wales, and there are centers throughout the country where craftsmen and women demonstrate their skills and sell their products, from glassblowing to wood turning, from weaving to needlework, from pottery to pewter work. Wool from Welsh sheep supports a significant woolen goods industry; and Welsh slate, which is very plentiful and still widely used for roofs, has proved a resource for craftspeople in a variety of end products from nameplates to figurines.

INTRODUCING NORTHERN IRELAND

The rich Scots-Irish brogue of Northern Ireland is unmistakable. While security, as far as the visitor is concerned, is generally not a problem, there are flashpoints from time to time, and it is therefore wise to avoid obvious taboo issues, such as religion and politics, in conversation. But as elsewhere on the island of Ireland you will receive a welcome warmer than most.

The Province of Northern Ireland (often called Ulster, although it includes only six of the nine counties of the former kingdom of Ulster) is inextricably linked to the heartbeat of British history. Geographically, it is part of the island of Ireland, although at its closest point it is separated from

Scotland by a mere 13 miles (21 km) of water, the North Channel.

After a bitter civil war, the famous national vote of 1921 offered the people of Ireland the choice between independence and self-rule, and remaining part of Britain. Twenty-six predominantly Catholic counties, including three from Ulster, chose independence, leaving only the six northern, and in those days largely Protestant, counties of Ulster to remain part of and loyal to Britain. For this reason they call themselves Loyalists (or Unionists).

Thus, there is a split culture in Northern Ireland, emanating from those associated with the Protestant tradition (principally Anglicans descended from the English settlers and Presbyterians from the Scottish settlers), who consider themselves British, and those associated with the Catholic tradition who consider themselves Irish. The two groups have a profoundly different mind-set.

GLIMPSES OF HISTORY

Archaeological evidence suggests a brief period of Roman occupation two thousand years ago. English history in Ireland goes back to the time of Henry II (1154–89), who in 1171 landed at Waterford with four thousand men and the blessing of Pope Adrian IV. Within weeks he had ensured that all the Irish bishops acknowledged the authority of Rome, and most of the Gaelic kings paid him homage.

In the generations that followed, a new feudal Ireland emerged, based on the Norman English model, complete with castles, manors, walled towns, monasteries, and a French-speaking knightly caste, which, according to one historian, was " . . . utterly unlike the cattle-droving, kinship-based clans of the indigenous Gaels."

The Plantations

In the seventeenth century, Ulster became home to major "plantations" involving Protestant settlers from England and Scotland, which, by definition, meant the confiscation of land. These were set up by James I from 1607 onward, following the failed Gunpowder Plot of 1605, which was blamed on the Catholics and which, in turn, gave rise to the hated anti-Catholic Penal Laws.

One of the most famous of these plantations was Derry, renamed Londonderry, because it was "adopted" by the City of London livery companies (these are charitable and professional associations that began as medieval craft and trade guilds, and accumulated great wealth and power). The livery companies took charge of building key areas of the city, from the town hall and the cathedral to quality properties and stately streets, in order to attract a new Protestant upper class that would govern the indigenous Catholic population. Unsurprisingly, much of the tortuous and tortured modern history of Ireland has its roots in this so-called "Plantation" period.

In 1641, just before the English Civil War, the Catholic Irish rebelled. They sided with the Royalists and were savagely suppressed by Oliver Cromwell, leader of the Parliamentary forces, whose name is loathed in the south.

The Protestant King

After the English forced James
II (1685–88), the last Stuart
king, who had converted to
Catholicism, to abandon
the throne, he fled to France
where he organized an army
and attempted to stage a
comeback. On July 12, 1690, the
new Protestant king, William of
Orange, defeated the Catholic French

and Irish forces under James at the Battle of the Boyne.
King Billy (as he was popularly known) and his white
horse are still to be seen painted on the sides of many
Belfast end-of-terrace houses.

The United Irishmen

In 1791, inspired by the American and French
Revolutions and seeking to turn Ireland into an
independent republic, a group of radical reformers
came together, calling themselves the Society of
United Irishmen. The French subsequently sent a
fleet of thirty-five ships to Bantry Bay to help them,
but the plan failed owing to bad weather. The
movement was suppressed after a failed rebellion in
1798. The Act of Union of 1800 abolished the Irish
parliament, and Ireland was incorporated into the
United Kingdom of Great Britain and Ireland in 1801.

The pity of it was that William Pitt, the English
Prime Minister, had promised various political
concessions to the Catholics as part of the Union deal.
But in the end, George III refused to sanction them,
saying that it would cause him to be disloyal to his
coronation oath to defend the Protestant religion if
he did so. Pitt resigned in protest.

TODAY'S POLITICAL LANDSCAPE

Northern Ireland has a 224-mile (360-km) border with the Irish Republic, forming the UK's only land boundary with another member state of the European Union. About half the population of 1.8 million live in the eastern coastal region, at the center of which is the capital, Belfast (population just under 300,000). Other major towns include Lisburn, Londonderry, Omagh, Antrim, and Bangor. There are twenty-six local government district councils, eighteen Members of Parliament elected to the House of Commons in Westminster, and, by proportional representation, three of the eighty-seven UK representatives elected to the European Parliament.

The planting of Scottish Protestant settlements and their Presbyterian culture among the indigenous Catholic population was always going to be problematic, as history has shown. A resolution of "The Troubles," as they are called, which began in the 1960s, is considered by many to have been concluded with the Good Friday Agreement and the reinstatement of the Northern Ireland Government in 1998, and with it the agreed power-sharing of the administration between Protestant and Catholic— the executive being managed by a First and Deputy First Minister.

The Northern Ireland Assembly sits in the Parliament Building at Stormont, in Belfast, and its 108 members have full legislative and executive powers. In the fall of 2002, however (for the second time), following a failure to reach consensus on aspects of the peace process, including the contentious issue of arms decommissioning, the Assembly was suspended, but was reinstated in May 2007 according to what was known as the St. Andrew's Agreement; powers relating to policing and justice were transferred in 2010. Following the British election of 2010, the fourth Assembly was convened in 2011.

Reunion with the Republic of Ireland continues to be an ideal for many Catholics in the north, and is the stated political objective of the radical Irish nationalist party, Sinn Fein. The 2011 census showed that the declared Catholic community and the declared Christian community (who were not Catholics) as almost the same at 41 percent each— with the Catholic community showing a slight increase and the non-Catholic community a slight decrease.

The Green and Orange Traditions

The most visibly challenging cultural aspect of the two traditions is dominated by the so-called marching season, which runs from Easter time to the end of September, and is essentially the preserve of the Protestant community. The biggest parades take place in July, marking the victory of William III, the Protestant King of England, over the Catholic forces under James II on July 11, 1690, at the Battle of the Boyne.

Such parades tend to be triumphalist in nature, featuring banners and bands, and are really a historical anomaly. They are mostly organized by Protestant/Unionist associations, including the "Orangemen" (who took their name from King William's family, the Dutch House of Orange) through their "Lodges." There is a Parades Commission that endeavors to strike a balance regarding time and place for parades; but parading appears to be an intractable problem.

The most visible manifestation of the "green" culture of the Catholic community is the wearing of the shamrock on St. Patrick's Day (March 17). Tradition holds that Ireland's patron saint used the three-petaled shamrock to illustrate the doctrine of the Holy Trinity. Shamrock is worn throughout Ireland on St. Patrick's Day, as it is in Irish communities all over the world.

THE NORTHERN IRISH ECONOMY

The Northern Ireland economy is the smallest of the UK regions, accounting for only 2 percent of total economic output, and continues to be a depressed economy, although there are encouraging signs of revival in both manufacturing and the services

sectors. Rural life is still a significant cultural factor in Northern Ireland, with agriculture, forestry, and fishing accounting for around 3 percent of GDP (compared to 1.2 percent for the UK as a whole). New inward investment supporting growth industries such as computer software and telecommunications and network services is highly prized as the old industries, such as shipbuilding at

Harland and Wolf in Belfast, have virtually disappeared, although H&W have restructured to become leading manufacturers of offshore wind power installations.

Linen Emblem

Belfast was famous as a center for high-quality linen, which was a significant part of the agricultural and manufacturing economies in the nineteenth century. Today this is remembered in the Northern Ireland Assembly, which features the linen or flax plant as its emblem—the six flowers signifying the six counties.

Some Famous Names

Irish culture, literature, and the performing arts in Ulster thrive as they do elsewhere. Well-known names in literature include Keith Baker, Colin Bateman, Jack Higgins, and C. S. Lewis; and the poets Ciaran Carson, John Hewitt, Louis MacNeice, and Seamus Heaney; in the acting profession star names include Colin Blakely, Kenneth Branagh, Amanda Burton, Liam Neeson, James Nesbitt, and Stephen Rea. In music, there are the flautist James Galway, singer/songwriter Van Morrison, pianists Phil Coulter and Barry Douglas, and blues guitarist Ronnie Greer. The world of golf celebrates the achievements of Darren Clarke and Rory McIlroy.

chapter three

VALUES & ATTITUDES

Given the great diversity of the British people, it is fair to ask what their shared values are. The answer to this can be found by looking at different contexts—the historical ethnic mix of British society, traditional religious beliefs, the class structure, and the emergence of a new, multicultural Britain.

In reality, there is no such a thing as a uniform "British culture"—it could only ever be English, Scottish, Welsh, Irish, or, indeed, Asian British, West Indian British (and so on) culture. The English, however, are by far the largest of these islands' peoples, and are culturally dominant. The main part of this chapter, therefore, and much that follows describes largely English characteristics— although there will be many that apply to all.

Some "Virtues" and "Vices"
The English love nature and creativity, order and harmony, language and wit; and dislike pomposity— having long removed themselves from any traditional culture of deference. They are naturally curious, they are tolerant and fair, modest, practical, resilient, and self-sufficient. They also love a good argument, confrontational debate rather than discussion, and cultivate fierce loyalties—

epitomized in the tribal support of local football clubs. They cherish their individuality ("my home is my castle") and celebrate idiosyncrasy, eccentricity, and the arcane. If asked, they might feel a "little bit British but mostly English."

But they can seem to appear "superior," exclusive, and reserved. They can be too fond of alcohol and the "pub culture," and anti-intellectual. They can be stubborn ("bloody-minded"), and skeptical.

In recent decades there have been a number of fundamental social changes—the blurring of the old class barriers being one of them. The emphasis placed on individual fulfillment during the Thatcher and Blair years prompted a huge expansion of entrepreneurial activity. This, combined with changing economic imperatives, resulted in a new culture of short-term employment contracts, which has led to very different notions, among working people, of loyalty, group responsibility, and perceptions of oneself in the community.

A SENSE OF IRONY

A British newspaper columnist once wrote that, after having been abroad for an extended period of time, it was an enormous relief to be back home in Britain and "on the same wavelength" as everyone else again. He put this down to reconnecting with the British sense of irony, one of the arteries of everyday communication.

Irony has to do with self-deprecation, with the "buzz" that comes from a tendency to laugh at oneself and one's situation, and an anticipation of constant, gentle amusement. Irony is a trigger for laughter, which, to paraphrase the Glaswegian comedian Billy Connolly, the British see as a form of free medication for body, mind, and spirit.

Just to complicate things further for the visitor, the English are also masters of the art of the understatement, and it is often the case that some of what they say is not quite what they mean. This is self-evident to the native listener, but with others it can cause misunderstandings. This particular aspect of the English character does not seem to travel well. (For example, someone who had managed to deal with an extremely difficult personal challenge or situation, when asked how hard it had been, might respond by saying "It was a bit tricky," or even, "It wasn't too bad.")

Not surprisingly, the British are not routinely polite to each other—a habit that can be oppressive in other cultures; and they don't suffer fools gladly. They are good "on parade," when they have to be, though they might grumble; but later they make merry, and usually make a good job of doing that too. Chaucer read the English character very well, and used irony, parody, and burlesque to great effect throughout the *Canterbury Tales*.

A SENSE OF TRUST

In his book *Trust*, Francis Fukuyama wrote of cultures that vary in fortune because of the levels of trust they enjoy and sustain; he cites Britain and Japan as High Trust cultures. It is certainly true that trust is implicit in the way the British manage their affairs, within local and central government, in their approach to law and order, including the principle that policing is done "with the consent of the people," in the way their judiciary system operates, and so on.

Trust is taken for granted in Britain, although it has been dented in recent times—by the exposure of hypocrisy in the political elite and the demise of conviction politics, and by other factors such as the revelations of child abuse linked to the churches, the new protocols evolving around new technology, the unknown landscape of the social media, and, for some, the tyranny of political correctness.

It is no surprise, therefore, that the degree of trust extended to each other in daily life is at times being sorely tested in what is essentially becoming a post-Christian society. The tradition of the "gentlemen's agreement" epitomized this philosophy of life and continues to be cherished, especially by the older generations committed to traditional values.

A SENSE OF FAIR PLAY

There is an old saying that "An Englishman's word is his bond," meaning as good as having a legal agreement. In other words, English society, which is not governed by a written constitution or a bill of rights, conducted itself on the basis of mutual trust and a sense of "fair play." For some, this is best

expressed in the national game of cricket. Although incomprehensible to most of the rest of the world (except the few other "Commonwealth" countries such as India, Sri Lanka, Australia, New Zealand, and South Africa that play it), cricket demands great skill and judgment, particularly on the part of the umpire, who must make key decisions on every ball bowled. It is all a matter of "fair play," and in fact the word "cricket," used in the sentence "it's not cricket," itself sums up the English idea of fairness.

In the late 1990s, the famous English cricket umpire Dickie Bird, now retired, was asked "what is Englishness?" He replied with the following key words: "beer, honesty, bulldog-type virtues, royal family, cricket, the weather." He also used the phrase "not giving up when things get tough." Answering the same question, Jeffrey Richards, Professor of Culture at Lancaster University, observed, "a sense of humor" and "a sense of superiority towards foreigners—not concealed." Another commentator mentioned "a stiff upper lip"—a tendency to put up with a bad situation without complaining, summed up in the working-class phrase, "Mustn't grumble."

KEEPING ORDER

The English expression that "there is a time and a place for everything," suggests a need for order. This can be seen in the way people automatically stand in line for public transport and other services; the order in the way the British conduct their civic and daily life; the requirement for "orderly conduct" at all times at public events—reinforced daily by the Speaker of the House of Commons, who calls (and sometimes shouts) "Order! Order!" (always twice) to silence over-excited Members of Parliament in the House of Commons.

Not surprisingly, this desire for order is reflected in the way the British have traditionally dressed. They still have a love of uniforms, especially those connected with the pomp and pageantry of a grand public occasion.

Even in everyday life there are many "uniform" traditions, in other words a need for uniformity in dress—often starting with school uniforms, obligatory at many schools, but particularly important at independent schools—hence the importance of wearing one's "old school tie" later in life at particular social functions in order to signal who you are and where you come from.

A SENSE OF IDENTITY

England, unlike Scotland and Wales, has no national costume. On the other hand, English customs and traditions involve a wide variety of costumes, from the pageantry associated with monarchy and great state occasions, through the distinctive red and black tunics worn by the Yeomen Warders (known as Beefeaters) who guard the Tower of London, to the traditional costumes worn by Morris Dancers at English country fairs.

So underplayed (or even undervalued) in England are the public displays of national identity—so highly prized elsewhere in the world—that England's national holidays do not

even include the feast of St. George (the patron saint of England, famous for slaying a dragon) on April 23. It used to pass unnoticed, but in recent times the United Kingdom Independence Party (UKIP) has made a deliberate effort to highlight its significance as part of English identity, whereas, as everybody knows, the celebrations by the Irish to mark the feast of St. Patrick on March 17 echo around the world.

The Welsh celebrate St. David's Day on March 1 and many wear one or both of the national emblems—a daffodil and leek—to mark the day, while schools organize special concerts.

A Sense of Superiority

This has been expressed as, "The rest of the world have to keep telling us how wonderful they are—like the French, Italians, or Germans, who imagine that a perfect world consists only of French, Italians, or Germans. But the English, who will mix with anybody, don't need to broadcast how good they are. They just *know* they're the best."

A SENSE OF FAIRNESS AND COMPROMISE

Tolerance, fair play, and an instinct for compromise
are fundamental qualities of the British character,
along with a strong sense of justice, which draws on
all of these and remains an abiding passion. Hence the
existence of the enormous number of charities in the
country, and the great amount of volunteer work done
in the community.

In more recent times, however, the consensus has
shifted from a sense of obligation to a new focus on
individual rights and self-interest, and the concern
for fairness that traditionally informed individual and
group behavior is less apparent. In turn, this attitude
has fed into "single issue" politics, which tend to
engage in extremes, such as the Animal Rights
movement or the ultra-right British National Party.
The British are also becoming a more litigious people.

ROYALTY, CLASS, AND "HONOURS"

Despite all the changes to the social, economic,
and legal landscape in the late twentieth and early
twenty-first centuries, it remains true to say that to

understand England and English ways (as opposed to Scottish, Welsh, or Northern Irish ways) you need to understand the class system. This continues to thrive. There are three main class divisions in England (which also apply in Scotland, but perhaps less so in Wales, whereas Northern Ireland has different social issues linked to sectarianism): upper class, middle class, and lower or working class. These are described in Chapter 7, Friendship, Family, and Social Life.

Until quite recently, everybody's perceived sense of "self" and their interpersonal relationships were informed by their view of their status within this class

structure. The royal family is essential to the survival of the class system, because it defines one's position in society. Without royalty there can be no new titles, therefore no acquiring of status, and therefore no public confirmation of one's place in society (other than the hierarchy of wealth prevailing in the USA and elsewhere). Over the centuries republicanism has come and gone in waves, but it has remained a minority sport.

As far as social behavior is concerned, it is generally true to say that the further up the social scale one goes, the more one will find people observing the old-fashioned conventions and formalities reflected in the old saying, "Manners makyth man."

Whatever recalibration of British society and its class structure may be taking place, however, "period drama" such as *Downton Abbey*, *Mr. Selfridge*, and *Jane Eyre*, which "celebrate" and highlight Britain's traditional class differences, continue to attract huge TV audiences. Does this speak to a deep-seated nostalgia for times past, with all its inequities, or is it just good entertainment? Perhaps something of both.

The "Honours" Lists

Britain has a public award system known as "honours," which confers recognition on worthy people for their contributions to society, from serving the country as diplomat, politician, or civil servant, to making outstanding contributions to industry, sport, and the arts, or simply for the good work an individual has done within their local community. In the 2015 New Year Honours List, a woman, aged eighty, was honored for her dedication over forty years as a "Lollipop Lady" providing safe crossing for children outside a primary school in North Wales. (The "Lollipop" is a "Stop" sign on stick used at a zebra– pedestrian—crossing.) There are a great many different levels within the honours system, but it means that people from all walks of life can aspire to elevation. It is also a benign way of co-opting talented people into the Establishment!

Not surprisingly, the grading of honours is very finely tuned, from peerages down to minor awards. The Honours Lists, as they are called, are announced twice a year and are known as the New Year's Honours and the Queen's Birthday Honours. The New Year list is largely compiled by the Prime Minister of the day, advised by ministers and civil servants. The Queen's Birthday list, although also drawn up under advice from ministers and civil servants, has some direct input from the Queen herself together with her counsel. Titles are so broadly conferred today that some people feel their inherent value has become debased. There are also members of the Labour Party who would like to see the entire system abolished.

RELIGION

England in both tradition and practice continues to be a Christian country, but has significant representations of other faiths, especially Muslim, Hindu, Sikh, and Jewish. The Catholic Church continues to have the largest adult active membership of any Christian denomination. In recent years, dwindling regular attendance at mass (less than one million) has been boosted by the arrival of immigrants from Eastern Europe and Asia, particularly Poland and the Philippines.

The Church of England, however, is the only established Church in Britain. Its head, the Archbishop of Canterbury, is appointed by the monarch on the advice of the Prime Minister of the day. Its members are known as Anglicans, and the

wider Anglican Communion (85 million worldwide), together with the Episcopal ministries, is represented in a total of 165 countries.

Denominational schools, such as Catholic and Church of England schools, are supported by the state in the same way as nondenominational schools. Easter and Christmas, the two most important events in the Christian calendar, are public holidays. At the same time, partly due to a more enlightened view of other faiths by schools and the media, festivals observed by other religions, such as Ramadan (Muslim), Diwali (Hindu), Vaisakhi (Sikh), and Passover (Jewish) are more widely understood and respected.

Churchgoing among Christians has dropped dramatically—to the extent that some observers are now wondering whether Britain as a whole has a majority of believers any more. However, religious organizations, including many multifaith groups, continue to be actively involved in volunteer work and the provision of social services. According to the 2011 census Christianity remains the major religion in Britain, followed by Islam, Hinduism, Sikhism, Judaism, and Buddhism, in that order.

In Britain as a whole, but in England in particular, the Protestant tradition has produced a wide-ranging architectural heritage. In a typical town, for example, you will see a variety of Protestant churches: Church of England, Methodist, Baptist, United Reformed, Plymouth Brethren, Salvation Army, Pentecostal, and Quaker (which are not so many compared to the three hundred or more different types of Protestantism to be found in the USA). As church attendance drops, or disappears altogether, many of these buildings become redundant and are converted for other uses, such as private dwellings, theaters, or community centers.

More recent developments within the Christian tradition have included the rise of the charismatic movement represented principally by Assemblies of God and the Pentecostal Churches.

A modest contribution to the spiritual dimension of life is provided by the BBC through its early morning "Thought for Today" broadcasts (in the Radio 4 *Today* program), to which spiritual leaders and others from different walks of life contribute by offering a short talk. (Some leading non-believers have argued that it is discriminatory not to invite them to speak on the program.) There is also BBC TV's weekly *Songs of Praise* program, from different churches throughout the country and including hymns, reflective thought, and a celebration of the history of the place. In 2010, civil ceremonies accounted for 68 percent of all marriages, reflecting a rising trend. Same-sex marriage was granted by Parliament for England and Wales in July 2013, and in Scotland in February 2014. No such legislation as yet exists in Northern Ireland.

A SENSE OF DUTY

Although today one hears stories of individuals and groups demanding their "rights," the individual desire to take part in volunteer work for the benefit of others remains a particular and remarkable trait of the British character. There are over 170,000 charitable organizations registered with the Charity Commission for England and Wales. In addition, thousands of other groups get together in support of local community activities and local needs in social welfare, education, sport, heritage, the environment, and the Arts. Annual national events such as Red

Nose Day (when thousands buy and wear a red plastic nose and do not mind looking ridiculous) in March, which is supported by the Independent Television (ITV), and Children in Need day in November, which is backed by a day-long program on the BBC, are the signals for millions of individuals, together with thousands of companies and community groups, to contribute money, time, and skill in entertainment or endurance projects to raise money for particular charities.

The "Sally Army"

Founded in London by William Booth in 1865, the greatly respected Salvation Army is today working in 126 countries and is one of the leading Christian organizations in Britain. After the government, it is the largest and most diverse provider of social services. These include hostel accommodation (offering more than three thousand beds every night for homeless people), work with alcoholics, anti human-trafficking work, a family-tracing service, older people's services, and children's and youth programs.

The arrival of the National Lottery in 1994 has had a negative impact on the amount of money given to charities; on the other hand, a significant proportion of the Lottery receipts goes to "good causes." But there are worries that the decline in participation in the Lottery (under 50 percent of households) at the start of the new century is a long-term trend, to the detriment of the good causes. On the other hand, gambling overall, including computer gambling, is on

the increase. According to the Gambling
Commission 57 percent of all adults take part in
some form of gambling on a regular basis, with
47 percent of participants buying National
Lottery tickets.

HIGH CULTURE OR LOW CULTURE?

Britain's is not a structured "high culture"
environment like the Netherlands, France, Italy,
Germany, and Austria, or for that matter the Czech
Republic, where the arts are the great benchmark of
civilized life and behavior, against which all other
levels of behavior are judged, and are all-consuming in
terms of finance, media interest, and general protocol.

Remarkably, the arts in Britain flourish, despite
insufficient support from the state, which, regardless
of the political party in power, has invariably taken
the somewhat philistine, anti-intellectual view that
money will be found only if it is deemed to be in the
national "cultural interest" at a particular point in
time, rather than as a matter of course. The great
British temples to the arts, such as the National
Gallery and the Royal Opera House in London, are

outstanding examples of their kind, but have always struggled to maintain their independence and obtain enough government funding to expand and experiment as they would wish. Happily, entrance to most public museums and galleries, including the British Museum, London, remains free.

The arts are often seen as divisive. Opera, for example, is widely perceived as being only for the rich, even though low-priced tickets are often available. The English love committees, so the government readily supports "quangos" ("quasi-autonomous nongovernmental organizations") such as the Arts Council, which is one of the conduits whereby the arts are managed and subsidized and appropriate compromises are reached; likewise the Sports Council and the Lottery Commission.

DRINK AND THE WORK ETHIC

In times past, the British were not known for applying themselves overconscientiously in the workplace: most worked simply to earn the money to live. Today, given the changing patterns and terms of employment, high levels of youth unemployment, so-called "zero hours contracts," and the significant numbers of EU citizens coming to work in Britain, the world of work is a very different place from what it was a generation ago. "Devotion to duty," and the very idea of "hard work" (with many honorable exceptions, not least EU workers from the former Soviet bloc who have outstanding reputations for hard work and good quality service) are not phrases that readily come to mind. Not surprisingly, following the cruel exploitation of labor during the Industrial Revolution, it was the British who established the world's first trade union movement to protect the rights of organized labor. In today's climate of economic rationalization and "perceived value for money," this attitude has also spread to the Civil Service, once a model of efficiency, and the public sector as a whole. One outcome of this situation is that Britain continues to struggle with improving productivity—that is output in man-hours invested, even though, at the time of going to press, the UK is the leading economy in Europe.

It has to be said that historically part of the problem, even going back to Chaucer's time, has been the love of alcohol—mostly in the form of ale, or today's beer, with wine now making huge advances. In 2014 the UK was the world's sixth-biggest consumer of wine after the US, France, Italy, Germany, and China. In fact, up to the middle of the twentieth century, England had more bars (known as "public houses," or "pubs") than any other country in the world. It was said that there was one on every street corner in every town in the land.

The Industrial Revolution was "lubricated" with alcohol; the great national projects, like the building of the railways and the docks of London and Liverpool, could not have been completed without it. Today, drinking continues to be part of the British way of life and excess drinking among young adults, including women, has been a developing problem for both the police and the health authorities. Some country pubs have suffered because of drinking and driving laws, but the pub continues to be at the heart of local communities. Pubs have also suffered because of the non-smoking legislation of 2006 (affecting all enclosed public places). Many have reinvented themselves as "gastro pubs," that is, as attractive places to eat good food as well as drink.

HUMOR AS ENTERTAINMENT

Humor, as we have seen, punctuates daily life, and is reflected in the wide variety of genres—situation comedy, sketch shows, stand-up, panel shows, and satire—available on TV and radio. Recent mainstream TV programs have included *Mock the Week*, *Room l01*, *Have I Got News for You*, *Mrs Brown's Boys*, *Miranda*, and *Live* [Comedy] *at the Apollo*. Sitcoms include several highly popular American imports, including *Friends*, *Seinfeld*, and *Frasier*. Cartoons such as *The Simpsons* also appeal—and not only to children! On radio, three of the most popular programs are *I'm Sorry, I Haven't A Clue*, *The Now Show*, and *Just A Minute*.

There is humor in cross-dressing—once a requirement for all drama in Shakespeare's time, but today found particularly in pantomime, where the classic family shows, such as *Jack and the Beanstalk*, *Cinderella*, and *Puss in Boots*, require that the "leading boy" (the hero) is played by a pretty girl and the "wicked stepmother" (the comic character) is played by a bulky, middle-aged man—the "pantomime dame."

The World of Amateur Dramatics

The British perhaps are instinctive Thespians: they love showing off (including the pomp associated with many public occasions), they love a challenge, they love "taking part," and are great individualists. No wonder, therefore, that the world of "amateur dramatics" (Amdram) continues to be very much alive and well in Britain. Up and down the country you will find local amateur dramatic societies putting on plays, musicals, and other entertainments. According to *The Independent* newspaper, in 2012 some 2,500 amateur dramatic groups around the country put on over 10,000 productions between them.

chapter four

THE MONARCHY, POLITICS, & GOVERNMENT

A BIRD'S-EYE VIEW

The visitor should know that Britain, which is regarded as the "Cradle of Democracy," is actually at odds with the rest of the developed world in that it does not have a written Constitution, in other words, at present the UK has no codified constitution, no single document that sets out the principles by which it is governed. Instead, laws and statutes are passed determining the nature of democracy and the freedoms enjoyed by the people as an ongoing process. Accordingly, legal justice is largely based on what is called the rule of precedent—in other words, what was determined in the past by way of legal ruling informs the present. Having said that, what is known as the Political and Constitutional Reform Select Committee of the House of Commons has been vigorously promoting the idea of a "New Magna Carta" and has been responsible for a consultation process with Parliament and the people that concluded on January 1, 2015.

Also, the whole apparatus of the legal system is steeped in history, including dress and court conventions, which mostly date back to the eighteenth and nineteenth centuries; this is clearly something that pleases the British, and there is no

sign of tradition being expelled. However, in the summer of 2003 the government announced it was going to do away with the Lord Chancellor's office— the oldest and most distinguished office of state in the land—and replace it with a Department of Constitutional Affairs. This is now in place and other fundamental reforms followed.

Thus, it is fair to say that October 1, 2009, marked a defining moment in the constitutional history of the United Kingdom: it was the date when judicial authority was transferred away from the House of Lords, and passed to a new Supreme Court for the United Kingdom in the historic setting of the former Middlesex Guildhall on Parliament Square. The Supreme Court is the final court of appeal in the UK for civil cases, and for criminal cases from England, Wales, and Northern Ireland. It hears cases of the greatest public or constitutional importance affecting the whole population.

If you are in London, it is well worth visiting the Public Gallery when the House of Commons is sitting in order to experience the "Mother of all Parliaments" firsthand.

England and Wales on the one hand, and Scotland on the other, continue as they did before the Act of Union (1707) to have a different system of law (including the police), a different judiciary, different education systems, different systems of local government, different national churches, and different government departments. As we have seen, since 1999 Scotland has had its own Scottish Parliament, while Wales has had a Welsh Assembly, with considerably fewer powers. Northern Ireland has also had its own self-government (Northern Ireland Assembly), which was returned to it in 2007. (See page 60.)

The World's Oldest Parliament

Interestingly, the world's oldest self-governing legislature is to be found in the Tynwald on the Isle of Man, which has been in continuous existence for over a thousand years. Originally under the nominal sovereignty of Norway until 1266, it came under the direct administration of the British Crown in 1765. It has two branches, the Legislative Council and the House of Keys, which sit separately to consider legislation, but also sit together in the capital, Douglas, and annually at St. John's, for other parliamentary purposes.

This recent process of "devolving power" also includes a change in London, where since 2000 there has been an elected mayor and a separately elected twenty-five-member Assembly (known as the Greater London Authority). In 2004 the Northeast of England held a referendum regarding devolving powers to a separate assembly, but overwhelmingly rejected the idea. However, following the Scottish Referendum in 2014, there are calls both within Parliament and in the country generally for devolved powers to be granted to England on the principle that there be only English votes for English laws.

THE QUEEN'S ROLE

The monarchy is the oldest institution of government in Britain. It can be dated back to Egbert, King of Wessex, who united England under his rule in 829. The only interruption to it was the short-lived republic, or Commonwealth, established by Oliver Cromwell, which lasted from 1649 till 1660. This brief experiment with republicanism was mourned by few.

The Queen's official title is "Elizabeth the Second, by the Grace of God, of the United Kingdom of Great Britain and Northern Ireland and of her other Realms and Territories Queen, Head of the Commonwealth, Defender of the Faith." The Queen is also Head of State of fifteen other

"Commonwealth realms," including Australia, New Zealand, Barbados, the Bahamas, Jamaica, Grenada, and the Solomon Islands, where she is represented by a Governor-General, appointed by her on advice from the ministers of the countries concerned and independent of the British government.

In legal terms, the Queen is head of the executive and therefore Head of State; she is an integral part of the government's legislature; she is head of the judiciary and commander-in-chief of all the armed forces of the Crown. She is also "supreme governor" of the established Church, the Church of England.

Royal Assent
When a Bill has passed through all its stages in Parliament, it is sent to the Queen for Royal Assent, after which it becomes an Act of Parliament and is part of the law of the land. Over the centuries, however, the monarch's absolute power has been almost eliminated, and the Queen acts on the advice of her government ministers. She gives audiences to her ministers (for example, she has a regular weekly meeting with the prime minister in which matters of state are discussed), she receives accounts of cabinet decisions, reads dispatches, and signs state papers. The UK, therefore, is governed by Her Majesty's government in the name of the Queen.

POLITICAL PARTIES
Broadly speaking, the political system in Britain is divided along class lines, although all parties would protest that they are founded on ideological principles. Thus, there is the Conservative and Unionist Party (Unionist is an inclusive word, but

also refers to the Protestant Unionist parties of Northern Ireland that support continued union with Britain), which has a history going back more than two hundred years. Historically, it saw itself as defending tradition, the landed gentry, and the middle classes; but in today's world of the politically uncommitted "floating voter," increased blurring of social distinctions, and challenges from the Labour Party, and more recently the UK Independence Party (UKIP), it appeals across the cultural spectrum.

The Conservatives are also referred to as "Tories"—originally a term of abuse meaning bandits, which emerged in the period of Charles II (1660–85). At the time, the other political faction was referred to as "Whigs" (today's Liberal-Democrats), meaning Scottish cattle thieves.

The Labour Party, founded at the end of the nineteenth century by the trade union movement, traditionally saw itself as the representative of the working classes. The former "Blairite" Labour Party (1997–2010), however, appealed, above all, to "Middle England"—the middle classes—which includes many "floating voters." But after losing the elections in 2010, it has sought to reconnect with its traditional working-class supporters.

The third major party is the Liberal Democratic Party, formed in 1988 when the Liberal Party, which also has roots going back over two hundred years, merged with the Social Democratic Party, formed in 1981. They occupy a position left of center, and appeal to the "high minded." The party campaigned for proportional representation in Parliament, and endeavors to make all decisions from the "moral high ground." After the general election of 2010 resulted in a hung parliament, the

Liberal Democrats joined the Conservatives in a coalition government, putting Liberals back in office for the first time in over seventy years. Conservative and Labour had each held office eight times since the Second World War.

Other Parties

Most significant, is the rise of the Scottish Nationalist Party (SNP), which dominates the Scottish Parliament and is expected to gain many seats from the Scottish Labour Party in the 2015 general election, which in turn may impact the balance of power if the election results in a hung parliament.

The UK Independence Party (UKIP), founded in 1993 by members of the Anti-Federalist League with the primary objective of securing the United Kingdom's withdrawal from the European Union, has become a significant alternative voice in British politics. In recent years, under the leadership of Nigel Farage, in addition to its primary objective of securing the UK's withdrawal from Europe, it is seeking to limit immigration into Britain. At the time of going to press it had secured two Members of Parliament (both of whom were originally members of the Conservative Party).

The Green Party, founded in 1990, currently has one MP, but has failed to make any significant impact on the conduct of British political life.

The Right of Self-Promotion

General elections to vote in a new government, which take place every four or five years, present an opportunity for the richly idiosyncratic nature of the English to display itself to the full, particularly in terms of the number of ridiculous and hopeless "minority" parties that spring up overnight. Most famous in recent years has been the Monster Raving Loony Party, created by the self-styled "Lord Sutch," who offered an alternative to anyone disgusted enough with the political system to give him their vote. According to the rules, however, any party (or individual) that puts itself up for election must also put up a cash deposit (currently £500), which is lost if it does not get a minimum of 5 percent of all votes cast.

ETIQUETTE OF THE "HOUSE"

It will come as no surprise to the reader to learn that Parliament is sustained by a great many conventions that go back centuries. For example, during debates in the House of Commons ("the House"), Members of Parliament (MPs) are not allowed to use each other's names; colleagues are called "My Honorable Friend" (or, if they are Privy Councillors, "My Right Honorable Friend"); whereas if they are opponents they are referred to as "the honorable gentleman (or lady)." There is no applause, and an MP can show only verbal agreement or dissent, hence shouts of "Here, here," which signify agreement.

Furthermore, there is a list of proscribed words in Parliament. Most importantly, you cannot call an honorable member a liar; but you could tell him you thought he was being "economical with the truth!"

The general manager of the House of Commons when it is "sitting," that is, in session, is the Speaker. He or she determines who shall speak, and maintains control during debates by calling out "Order! Order!" when members become too noisy. Were the Speaker to stand up at any time because of serious disorder, then all members are obliged to sit down.

chapter five

FOOD &
DRINK

British cooking has been much maligned. There are some stereotypical ideas about it that may be partially true. For example, it has been said that the Puritans of the seventeenth century cast a shadow over just about every aspect of English life, leaving only a faint memory of the traditions of "Merrie England" that predated them. For a time, food, or the love of it, may not have escaped this shadow. But, as amply demonstrated below, that shadow has long passed and has been replaced by a new exuberance and fascination with food in the twenty-first century.

It is also worth noting that the years of austerity and sometimes poverty during the Second World War (and the years immediately following the war's end) also had a considerable impact on food choices and expectations. Most people simply had to "make do"— in many cases ingeniously—with whatever they could get, or could grow for themselves. The catchphrase "Dig for Victory" was widely used and encouraged people and families to be as self-sufficient in vegetables as possible. By way of inspiring others, King George Vl even turned some of the flowerbeds at Buckingham Palace into vegetable plots. As a result, the British people became used to second-best for a while. The actor John Cleese, famous for his role in the sitcom *Fawlty Towers*, recalls how, for his parents, the only thing that mattered at the dinner table was that the plates were hot. The quality of the food was of secondary importance.

Despite the stories and the stereotypes, British food, at its best, has actually always been tasty and wonderfully varied. The fertile land and temperate climate, suitable for both agriculture and livestock, yielded fine-quality meats, game, crops of cereals and vegetables, and an abundance of delicious fruits. Surrounded by water, Britain had plentiful stocks of a great variety of fish and seafood. Trade with countries all over the world brought hot, mild, and aromatic spices, and welcome "new" foods such as potatoes, oranges, bananas, and pineapples. Britain had all the ingredients, and became skilled at preparation, producing a great variety of cheeses (many of which today are exported to countries around the world, including France), smoked and cured meats and fish, along with its own favorite dishes such as roast meats, poultry, and game, nourishing soups and gently simmered stews, Yorkshire pudding, steak and kidney pie, Lancashire hotpot, shepherd's pie, fruit pies, and steamed puddings. British beer, cider, and "scotch" are well known for their quality. Sometimes British food has been described as "bland," but this is hardly true today. In any event, British food has always been enhanced by the use of hot, sharp, or spicy additions—mustard, vinegar, horseradish, pepper, pickles, and chutneys.

In modern times, what lost Britain its reputation as a food-loving nation was, primarily, the food that was available in institutions and restaurants, which for many years, until the late 1960s, generally lacked the imagination and drive to produce the kinds of meals to tempt people to eat out more than they had to. The British did not have a strong tradition of dining out for pleasure. Then things started happening: people began traveling overseas to new holiday destinations and in so doing discovered other foods; they wanted to eat out more, and demanded something better. Gradually, more restaurants opened up in the cities, and with this added competition and impetus the whole restaurant culture started to improve.

Over time, food programs began to appear on television, leading to a point today where food— either in a competitive cooking environment or simply as how-to programs—is the central focus of a wide array of TV shows, such as *Masterchef*, *Professional Masterchef*, *The Great British Bake-Off*, *Ready Steady Cook*, and *River Cottage*. So-called "foodies" such as Jamie Oliver, Gordon Ramsay, Delia Smith, Keith Floyd, and Nigella Lawson became known internationally. The media explosion in this area is a phenomenon. Indeed, cookbooks have for some time outsold the Bible. Nevertheless, it is ironic that such programs appear to be viewed largely for their entertainment value with little evidence that "cooking inspiration" is being transferred to the domestic kitchen, as eating out, instant food, and "take-aways" (food "to go") continue on an upward trend.

Today, restaurants in London and the major cities serve English and international cuisine to the highest standards. Eating out is increasingly common, driven in part by greater personal wealth and the fast-food culture of youth, but also by the tendency among busy professional people not to cook very much at home, preferring after a long day's work to relax over a meal cooked by someone else.

This "discovery" of the taste and variety of food has also seen a huge increase in Britain's Indian and Chinese restaurants—Indian being the biggest "foreign" food of choice—so much so, that an annual competition for the finest Indian cook in the land has been celebrated on television for a number of years, and it has been said that Britain's favorite food is chicken *tikka masala*!

The "Fish and Chips" Story

The British love freshly made chips from real potatoes, which for the *aficionados* are very superior to the processed "French fries" served by the fast-food chains. Fish-and-chip shops as we know them today first appeared in the 1860s, and expanded rapidly, thanks to the first steam trawlers that quickly brought in quantities of fish from the North Atlantic and the waters around Norway and Iceland. Their clientele was the massive workforce employed by Britain's ever-expanding industries.

The National Federation of Fish Friers (established in 1913), which represents the largest take-out food trade in Britain, estimates there are currently over 10,000 specialist fish-and-chip shops in the UK, and that over 50 percent of the population buy fish and chips as a family meal on a regular basis.

The traditional favorite fish is cod, although it is now the most expensive because of diminishing fish stocks, and haddock and plaice follow in popularity, along with local fish. The "chippy" will also sell you such alternatives as chicken, steak or chicken pies, or sausages, or kebabs, all with chips—or, indeed, just chips on their own. Always on hand, for any or all of these, are salt and vinegar—essential flavorings for a true fish-and-chip meal—or tomato ketchup or "brown sauce" (see below). Fish and chips were traditionally wrapped in newspaper; today's hygiene laws insist on approved paper and/or paper boxes.

Home Comfort

Sales may be falling, but the famous brown sauce, HP Sauce, which has a ketchup-type consistency, continues to be consumed in great quantities; those who use it like its "bite"—the ingredients include malt, tomatoes, molasses, and vinegar. Registered by a Nottingham grocer in 1895, but today manufactured by the Heinz company in the Netherlands, it is apparently consumed in the highest circles: HP Sauce is honored by a Royal Warrant!

MEALS OF THE DAY
The Great British Breakfast

Hotels, guesthouses, and cafés throughout the country continue to serve a "full English breakfast" to those who want it. You will be offered fruit juice or cereals, and then some or all of the following, most of which are fried or grilled (broiled): bacon, eggs, sausages, sautéed potatoes, tomatoes, mushrooms, kidneys, black pudding, and baked beans, eaten with toast and butter. To this challenging plateful, those who are sauce-dependent may also add tomato ketchup or brown sauce. The meal is completed with more toast, butter, and marmalade (and /or jams), and tea or coffee.

Porridge or cold cereals, eggs cooked in any way, ham, smoked fish, such as kippers (actually smoked herrings), or kedgeree—a rice and smoked haddock dish, a tradition going back to the days of the British in India—are all good British breakfast fare. There is always, as an alternative, the "Continental" breakfast, consisting of orange juice, bread rolls, cold meats, hard-boiled eggs, toast, or croissants, with jam, and tea or coffee.

These days, most people do not eat the full English breakfast, preferring a quicker and lighter meal of cereals and toast, at any rate during the week. What continues to survive, however, is traditional English marmalade. Made from oranges (sometimes other citrus fruits) and sugar, this is available in different versions, from a sweet, jelly-type preserve to a thick, dark variety incorporating chunks of cooked orange peel. Many people make their own marmalade once a year, usually in late January, when the bitter Seville oranges from Spain are available.

Lunch—and Brunch
Some families (mostly northern or working class) refer to the midday meal as "dinner," as do schools throughout the land. For the middle and upper classes, however, the midday meal is "lunch."

Then there is "brunch," which replaces breakfast and lunch, typically on weekends when you have not had to get up early, or have already been out for a swim or a jog. It is a relaxed, informal meal of whatever you fancy, and would be eaten around 11:00 a.m.

Lunch for working people during the week tends to be of the "soup, sandwich, or salad" variety. It is usually a light meal, though restaurants serve two or three courses for those who want them. Children would usually have their main meal of the day at this time.

A traditional English Sunday lunch typically has just two courses: the "main" course—usually meat or poultry (lamb, beef, pork, or chicken), normally roast, or perhaps slowly cooked in a casserole, accompanied by potatoes and probably two other vegetables. Over the roast meat is poured gravy, made from the meat juices, or from an instant mix. The second course may be called "pudding," "sweet," or "dessert," and is often some kind of pastry in the form of a tart or pie, filled with fruit; or even an old-style English dish such as sponge or bread-and-butter pudding. Over this may be poured cream or custard, a sweet sauce, traditionally made from eggs, sugar, and milk, flavored with vanilla, but nowadays often made from a powder or bought ready-made. In the health-conscious modern world, cheese and fruit are often eaten as an alternative to "pudding."

Tea

In the late 1930s, the drinking of tea was celebrated in the song "A Nice Cup of Tea" from a musical called *Home and Beauty*. The first lines of the second stanza read: "I like a nice cup of tea with my dinner and a nice cup of tea with my tea . . ."

Tea is a great British institution, though visitors should be aware that the term can be confusing. "Tea" can be just a cup of tea, or it can mean a light meal. For example, the Victorian and Edwardian upper classes enjoyed an agreeable social ritual at 4:00 p.m.

This consisted of tea to drink, plus a generous array of sandwiches, cakes, and tarts, and this is still an accepted way of entertaining, particularly on weekends. Many London hotels, including the Ritz

and Claridges, are famous for their teas, and sometimes offer variations such as "Champagne Afternoon Tea". At its most basic level, "tea" consists of a cup of tea (with perhaps a biscuit) sometime in the afternoon.

A delicious variant is a "cream tea," which consists of scones with jam and the thick clotted cream that is a specialty of the West Country (Devon and Cornwall), though now widely available elsewhere.

The term "high tea" can mean an early cooked meal for the family after school and work—the last cooked meal of the day. It is also occasionally used to mean "afternoon tea."

Supper or Dinner?

Supper is a simple family meal eaten at any time in the evening that is convenient. During the week it may consist of a cooked dish, such as lamb chops, cottage pie (minced meat is the main ingredient, topped with mashed potatoes and cooked in the oven), or, these days, pasta, followed by cheese and fruit. If there is more time to spend on preparation, supper may be a more elaborate meal, but the name implies informality.

The word "dinner" usually describes a more formal evening meal, typically starting between 7:30 and 8:30 p.m., and involving guests or dining out in a restaurant. It consists of three or more courses, and a special effort would be made both in the preparation of the food and in the table setting. It will usually be preceded by an alcoholic drink—spirits or wines—and there will be wine with the meal, perhaps a different one with each course.

INVITATIONS

Invitations to a meal in someone's house, even "dinner," will usually mean a relaxed, lighthearted occasion. More often than not these days, men (particularly younger men) do not wear business suits or ties on these occasions; they would probably have changed into something smart but casual. Women probably wear elegant but comfortable rather than very glamorous evening clothes (which they might wear for a "black tie" event).

It is usual to take a gift, such as flowers, a box of chocolates, or wine. These do not have to be very expensive, but they should be attractive and of good quality. Do not buy flowers from a gas station! The wine may not be opened, if particular wines have been chosen to go with the meal, but it will be appreciated.

It is polite to send a short note of thanks after such an occasion. Some people prefer to telephone the following day. Do one or the other. The younger generation will communicate by text or social media.

TABLE MANNERS

A French saying suggests that, "While the English have good table manners, the French know how to eat." It is certainly true to say that, generally speaking, while the Englishman attempts to push peas on to his fork, the

Frenchman turns the fork upside down and uses it more as a spoon, thus accelerating the process of eating and enjoying—albeit without scoring highly on etiquette.

The British continue to use a knife and fork in the traditional way. Both are held while eating, the fork, with the prongs facing down, in the left hand, and the knife in the right, and in polite circles they are rested on the plate between mouthfuls, or for a break for conversation. Some young people are adopting the American habit of cutting up all their food first and then eating it with just the fork; though traditionalists view this as "not correct," and childish. If nothing on the plate requires cutting, then it is acceptable to use only a fork, held in the right hand. A spoon and fork are used for eating pasta, including spaghetti.

Unlike the French custom, English children were traditionally brought up to rest their hands in their lap; later you were allowed to put your wrists on the table; but putting your elbows on the table, and, worst of all, resting your chin on your hands, were definitely not allowed. The idea was that you should not flop about lazily over the table, and this sort of behavior would elicit the remark, "Do you feel ill? Would you like to lie down?" Nowadays these manners are less strictly adhered to, except on formal occasions.

EATING OUT

Given today's much more liberal attitude to dress when eating out, it is important to be sure whether or not the establishment you are going to insists that men wear a tie. A tie continues to be demanded by traditional London clubs, such as the Garrick, the Reform, and the Athenaeum.

Usually, when you are sent an invitation to a formal lunch or dinner, the dress code will be noted on the card, for example, "lounge suit," or "black tie," which means "dinner jacket" (tuxedo). This code will automatically determine the dress code for the women.

Food On Your Plate—The Unwritten Rule

The British never cease to be amazed at the quantities of food served in America; equally, American visitors to Britain are often astonished at the small amounts of food that are put on their plates. In Britain, the rule used to be to eat everything on the plate, whether you or somebody else had put it there, as it was thought to be wasteful to leave anything uneaten. Now this has relaxed somewhat—if it's too much, leave it—but only in a restaurant, not in someone's house. If you are not very hungry, ask for a small helping.

The English and Service

Visitors should understand that basically the English today do not like serving others: it is seen as rather demeaning, which perhaps is a legacy from the rigid class structure of the old days. The situation is not helped by the fact that the service industry as a whole is also the lowest-paid sector in Britain.

In other societies there is no such baggage from the past, and service is seen as something positive. Thus, it is increasingly foreign workers who populate the service industry in Britain today. Indeed, there is hardly a hotel, restaurant, bar or any other venue countrywide where service is required that does not employ staff from Eastern Europe, especially Poland and the Baltic states of Lithuania, Latvia, and Estonia.

Paradoxically, there has also been a degree of rehabilitation of the service industry through a resurgence of interest in becoming a housekeeper, nanny, or butler, as more and more couples, with both partners pursuing professional careers, find they cannot cope without such help.

TIPPING

Traditionally, a tip of 10 percent, or slightly more, has been left for the waiter or waitress, regardless of the quality of food or service. It is an easy policy just to stick to this, particularly in a formal situation. But, increasingly, there has been a move against such automatic generosity, particularly among younger people. In the final analysis, you make your own decision, although good manners dictate that whatever you do, particularly if you are entertaining guests, you should not embarrass anybody. Sometimes a "service" charge is added to the bill, which solves the problem if you are prepared to pay it, as most people do.

THE PUB

Despite the rigorous drink-driving laws and the no-smoking ban, for many British people the pub continues to be the center of their social lives—amply demonstrated in the ongoing soaps of *Coronation Street* and *Eastenders*. Typically, people will pop in for "a quick one," which means a pint of beer; or "a swift half," which also means a pint of beer! Some serious drinking men spend the evening there, "propping up the bar."

Pubs often have interesting old names that in some way reflect their history, like the Queen's Arms, the Woolpack, the Red Lion, the White Horse, the Eight Bells, the Victoria, the Green Man, the Ship Inn, the Boot and Flogger, the Bunch of Grapes. The variations are endless, and typically you will find the pub's name painted on a sign swinging by the front door or on a post nearby. The Tabard in Southwark, London, for example, was mentioned by Chaucer in the *Canterbury Tales* six hundred years ago, and Ye Olde Cheshire Cheese, in Fleet Street, London, was frequented by some of England's literary giants, including Samuel Johnson, Oliver Goldsmith, and Charles Dickens.

As part of the rise of youth culture in Britain in the 1990s (a culture that has continued its momentum well into the twenty-first century), some pubs were rebranded to appeal to smart and well-off young singles. Some of the old-fashioned names, such as

Pig and Whistle or Royal Oak, went, and the pubs were refurbished with a "cool" new look; one of these new chains is called the Slug and Lettuce, in a tongue-in-cheek echo of the old names.

The most enduring image of the pub, however, is that of the country pub, which continues to be the heart of village life, although according to CAMRA (Campaign for Real Ale) in 2014 pubs were closing at the rate of one a day, leaving a total of some 55,000 throughout Britain. Some have been there for hundreds of years; some have thatched roofs with wisteria or roses growing around the doorway. There are blazing log fires in winter, and an attractive garden to sit in for the summer months. These can be delightful, welcoming places, with "regulars" at the bar who are often only too happy to chat with visitors.

Traditional English beer has made a big comeback in recent years, sufficient to encourage the establishment of many new small independent breweries to serve their local area. Brewed from malt and hops, it is not refrigerated like other beers, which is why those who do not know when it is at its best (cooled but not chilled) criticize it for being "warm" beer, in contrast to the sometimes teeth-chilling temperature of pressurized or cask beer—principally lager, the lighter Continental beer. One of the most famous darker bitter beers is Newcastle Brown, drunk mostly in the northeast of England where it is made, and favored by football supporters and many others.

If you go into a pub and ask for "a pint of best" you will be served with what the publican rates as "best bitter"; these days, though, there is usually a choice of several English beers, possibly including a local brew, plus Continental-style lagers, which are served chilled. There is also "mild" beer, drunk mostly in the Midlands, which is what its name suggests—a beer brewed from hops but not as sharp as bitter, and softer on the palate—and never chilled!

Public and Saloon Bars

Many pubs continue to be divided into sections, such as the public bar, which is thought to be noisier, more "working class," and where the beer used to be perhaps a penny a pint cheaper than in the neighboring saloon bar, which is meant to be quieter and more salubrious. There is sometimes a smaller room called a "snug," where there may be an open fire. On the other hand, many pubs have now lost all the dividing walls in favor of one large drinking area for everyone.

Country pubs in some places have preserved some of the traditional "Olde England" games, such as "bat-and-trap" (found in Kent), which have been played for hundreds of years, or "shove ha'penny."

Pub games continue to be very popular, especially darts, and quizzes, both of which are frequently organized on a competitive basis.

Food is another essential component of the pub scene; once pub food was limited to very basic and cheap fare like pie or sausage and chips, or cheese and pickle ("Ploughman's Lunch" is now a much more elaborate version of this, with fresh bread and salad). Today is it recognized that people want good-quality food, and in most pubs there is now a much greater choice at reasonable prices. Some establishments have set out to offer restaurant-quality cuisine, and from this have created a new style of "pub culture." These are known as "gastro pubs."

Licensing Laws

The minimum age for drinking alcohol in Britain is eighteen, and the minimum age for entering a public bar (for consuming nonalcoholic drinks) is fourteen, but only if accompanied by an adult. Pubs that serve lunches may show families with children into a special dining room.

The government, however, continues to review licensing laws. "Opening hours," as they are called, used to be strictly observed: from 11:00 a.m. until 2:30 p.m., and from 5:30 p.m. until 11:00 p.m. (and a shorter time on Sundays). Now, publicans are free to stay open all day and all night if they wish; but outside city centers the old closing hours tend to prevail.

Typically, those serving in a pub will sound a bell at least ten minutes before closing so that last orders can be taken. Extension to the licensing laws can be granted by the local magistrate if a publican can demonstrate there is a justifiable special occasion, such as a World Cup match, or a spectacular royal wedding, which can be viewed on the pub's large-screen television.

WINE BARS

These are generally found in the city centers. Many of them are very attractive places, some being refurbishments of old pubs, some ultramodern. Most of their clients are professional people having a quick lunch or a more leisurely supper; such places provide a good environment to meet a friend or business associate for a casual meal. They offer a variety of interesting wines, and usually very good food. Wine is not compulsory! Soft drinks and coffee are also available.

chapter six

TIME OUT

For the British today, leisure and pleasure are a major preoccupation, wonderfully summed up in the saying "TGIF"—"Thank God It's Friday!" Indeed, even on a Monday, with the previous weekend just past, broadcasters and the printed media are already heralding the joys to come for the following weekend, creating a seamless year-round perception that life is all to do with having a ball— just a pity there is the work thing getting in the way!

The cultural scene is certainly vibrant, and there has been a renaissance in the public interest in art galleries and museums of all kinds, led by the British Museum (6.7 million visitors in 2013), the National Gallery (6 million), the Natural History Museum (5.3 million,) and Tate Modern (4.8 million), with new galleries, such as the Turner Gallery in Margate, and the Staffordshire Hoard gallery at the Birmingham Museum and Art Gallery (featuring the largest hoard of Anglo-Saxon gold ever found), springing up in towns and metropolitan centers across the country—in part thanks to proceeds from the National Lottery. Overseas visitor numbers of course have also been increasing.

The British love of language continues to find expression in theaters large and small, including local amateur dramatic societies (see page 81), as well as in summer-season variety shows (including comedians, singers, and magicians) in the country's leading coastal resorts—perhaps the most famous of all being Blackpool, with shows staged at its famous Tower. The pantomime (see page 81), a unique family entertainment in the Christmas vacation period, also flourishes. London's "Theatreland'" in the West End comprises some forty theaters—the longest-running show being Agatha Christie's *The Mousetrap*, now in its sixty-third year (2015).

POMP AND PAGEANTRY

The ceremonials of great public occasions continue to exert a hold on the imagination of the British, and are as much an attraction for them as for visitors from abroad. The State Opening of Parliament, for example, is a grand form of public theater. The Queen travels to the Palace of Westminster in a magnificent horse-drawn state coach, and, dressed in her royal robes, delivers a speech from the throne

of the House of Lords. Around her the assembled ranks of lords, ladies, judges, and officers of the House are arrayed in splendid ermine-lined red robes, gowns, or uniforms, the military in the dress uniforms of their regiments with all medals on display, and the members of "the other place" (the House of Commons) in formal "morning suits."

Especially impressive is the spectacular Trooping the Colour, when the Queen, as Commander-in-Chief of the Armed Forces, accepts her new regiment of guards, in full dress uniform, to mark her "official birthday" on the second Saturday in June. Other great spectacles include the procession of the Judiciary to the Law Courts of the Old Bailey in London, at the start of a new law term; and other state occasions when the Queen rides in one of the luxurious, horse-drawn carriages along the Mall (the road in front of Buckingham Palace), with guards on horseback in attendance.

WHERE TO GO AND WHAT TO DO

London is a world center for the arts and its theater options are legendary. In addition to the world-class museums and art galleries mentioned above, there are many other fascinating museums in and around London, for example the Design Museum, London Transport Museum, the Imperial War Museum, and the National Maritime Museum (NMM) at Greenwich—all of which offer free access. At Greenwich, in addition to NMM, there is the Queen's House (a former royal residence used by Anne Boleyn, Henry VIII's second wife) and the Royal Observatory, founded in 1675 by Charles II, and home of Greenwich Meridian (zero degrees

longitude), which determines Greenwich Mean Time. The Maritime London gallery is a permanent exhibition exploring the importance of London's maritime heritage and its impact on world trade.

Visitors should plan well ahead to see the choice available of any of London's shows and events, and book in advance whenever possible.

Beyond London, there is a wealth of heritage, arts, and history to discover in the main metropolitan centers and regions of England, including one of the new "wonders of the natural world," the Eden Project in Cornwall; the Royal Botanic Gardens, Kew; Portsmouth Historic Dockyard where Nelson's flagship "Victory" in the Battle of Trafalgar (1805) is on display; Kelvingrove Art Gallery and Museum,

Glasgow; the Ashmolean Museum, Oxford; Titanic Belfast; and Shakespeare's Birthplace, Stratford on Avon. Information is available through the regional tourist boards.

Some Formal Occasions and What to Wear
Ascot is one of the country's leading horse-racing venues and is famous for the "Royal Ascot" races in June, when the Queen attends for the Gold Cup (usually with one of her horses taking part). Unsurprisingly, the "Royal Ascot" week is also famous for the fact that it is a notable society fashion occasion, at which women show off their clothes, especially their hats. It attracts wide media interest.

On the other hand, the traditional Englishman watching the national summer sport of cricket at Lord's cricket ground in London, the home of the game, will wear the exclusive club tie of the home club, the Marylebone Cricket Club (MCC), together with a Panama hat, and even a blue blazer, regardless of how hot it is.

Equally, if you are attending the Royal Regatta at Henley (on the first weekend of July), particularly if you are a member of the very exclusive Leander Rowing Club, dress protocol demands that you wear an appropriate shirt and tie.

"Cool Britannia"

In recent times, British fashion designers have gained increasing prominence in the world of *haute couture*. This has led to a resurgence of the notion of "Cool Britannia" across society, which in turn has forced change on many major chains and suppliers in the clothes industry who were losing contact with their public. For example, at the end of the 1990s and again in 2011 Marks & Spencer had to reinvent itself by employing some top names in fashion to "rethink" its product lines (including the famous "St. Michael" brand of lingerie). Other brands, such as Next, Monsoon, Primark, and Miss Selfridge have surged ahead.

Fashion, of course, is very much part of "lifestyle," and has quickly fed into contemporary expectations of behavior and etiquette, for example, in eating out. Apart from notable exceptions in London such as the Ritz Hotel, and the traditional gentlemen's clubs of Pall Mall, St. James's, and Piccadilly, smart casual wear (not a suit and tie, except perhaps for business lunches/dinners) when eating out is now the norm.

Inevitably, this new, "no rules," supposedly relaxed dress code in public leads to widespread variations in interpretation. "Smart casual" for one man could mean a patterned T-shirt, jeans, and sneakers; for another it could mean a polo-necked sweater with black trousers and leather shoes.

"CASUAL" IS GOOD

"Casual," which projects the idea of being cool, relaxed, and at ease, is the new chic in today's society. By definition, such an attitude challenges the formal behavior of earlier generations, which was characterized by the notion of the "stiff upper lip," of not giving into one's emotions in the face of difficulties.

The royal family has also embraced a "casual" and more informal approach in recent years— particularly well demonstrated by the highly successful opening ceremony of the 2012 London Olympics, when the Queen was filmed meeting James Bond in Buckingham Palace, and later (apparently!) leaping out of a helicopter with a parachute to land in the Olympics stadium. Likewise, the more informal approach adopted by the Duke and Duchess of Cambridge as regards managing the media interest in motherhood and family life, including their tour of Australia in April 2014 with the infant Prince George, is widely appreciated. The Queen's 2014 Christmas Day Message, which focused on reconciliation, was the most-watched program of the day, attracting 7.8 million viewers.

SHOPPING

Shopping can be both a chore and a pleasure, depending on what you are buying. In towns and cities, supermarkets of all sizes generally supply the week's basic food needs, and there are smaller, specialist shops of all kinds. (Note that a "chemist"— an unfamiliar term to many visitors—sells drugs and medicines, along with all kinds of toiletries and

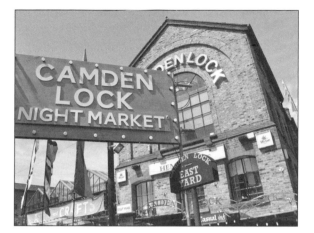

perfumes.) Many villages still have their own "village shop," or general store, that sells a huge variety of goods and often doubles as a post office—but sadly these continue to dwindle in number. Markets for fresh food and other items regularly take place in many towns. These typically offer good value.

Vast out-of-town shopping malls are also a feature of modern life, providing the opportunity for a day out for many families. Among the best known are Bluewater in north Kent, the biggest of its kind in Europe, comprising 330 stores that attract some 38 million visitors a year. In pole position for visitor numbers is West Stratford City, London, which attracts nearly 50 million visitors a year. Many of London's world-famous stores, such as those in Knightsbridge, Piccadilly, and Bond Street, are magnets for style-conscious shoppers.

As for souvenirs from Britain, there are as many choices as there are regions and major attractions. Traditional choices include fine woven woolen goods from Scotland and Wales down to sweet treats such as Scottish shortbread and Edinburgh rock, fudge and toffee, and, of course, marmalade. The choices in trinkets and mementoes in London are vast and various, many predictably featuring the Union Jack, the Houses of Parliament, and Buckingham Palace.

It is also interesting to seek out the old and unusual, and in all the cities and in countless country towns you can spend hours browsing for anything from antique silver, furniture, and paintings to secondhand books and "junk." Britain seems to have an almost endless supply of such items, from quaint and quirky, through attractive and affordable, to unique and costing a fortune. Many towns also have regular antiques fairs and flea markets, as well as boot fairs, which often offer real bargains and are well worth a visit. Television programs, such as the BBC's *Antiques Roadshow*, *Flog It!*, *Bargain Hunt*, and *Cash In The Attic*, are great entertainment and hugely popular, and no doubt help energize the antiques trade generally.

"By Royal Appointment"

Official suppliers of goods and services to the royal family receive a special kind of patronage. They can apply for a royal warrant permitting them to display a sign that they are "By Royal Appointment . . ." for example, " . . . suppliers of provisions and household goods to Her Majesty the Queen" or " . . . outfitters and saddlers to HRH The Prince of Wales." Find this on a jam jar, and you know you are eating well!

SPORTING LIFE

Though not for generations masters of so many of the sports they invented—including cricket, tennis, and football (with some honorable exceptions)—the British are obsessed with the sporting life. In an age of the cult of personality the homage paid at the altars of the sporting gods is almost without precedent.

Football

Football (soccer), above all, has even been described as the "new religion," driven by the multimillion-pound clubs of the Premier League, dominated in recent times by Manchester City, Chelsea, and Manchester United.

Thankfully now mostly free of the hooligan element (at least in home matches) and mob violence, the traditional working-class interest in football has given way to a complete cross-cultural involvement, with greater numbers of women and families watching the games than ever before. The same applies to rugby football, whether League or Union (the latter until recent years being played by nonprofessionals, and which always claims to be the true game).

"Being a good loser" is most noticeably (but not exclusively) linked to English middle-class culture, which applauds everyone for taking part, even if the game ends in defeat. In other words, winning is not necessarily the main point. This emphasis on the value of joining in, or taking part, reinforced through schools, especially the private schools, goes back for generations. In some ways, it is akin to the community spirit that is seen in times of war or disaster. It is hardly surprising, therefore, that the so-called "killer instinct" needed to win at sport is rarely developed enough in British players for them to beat the rest of the world.

Cricket
It might be argued that only the quiet, thoughtful persona of the English could have invented a game that can take up to a whole day or, in the case of Test cricket, up to five days, to complete. Self-evidently, it is a serious game, a game of endurance, commitment, and application. Even so, it is actually meant to be fun too. It is fun because everybody in the team takes part either batting or fielding (and for some, bowling), and usually everybody gets the chance to hit the ball and score runs. Taking part, or "having a go," is important.

Cricket is also a game demanding fair play by the umpire and players. Put in its simplest form, a very hard ball is hurled (correctly described as "bowled") at the wicket (consisting of three wooden stumps) in front of which a player from the other team is holding a wooden bat. His job is to stop the ball hitting the wicket (and himself), and to score "runs" by hitting the ball as far as possible and running fast, a "run" being the act of running the distance between the wickets at each end of the pitch—the traditional 22 yards (just over 20 meters). The other batsman from the same team, positioned at the other end of the pitch, has to run also, and both must return to their positions at the wickets before the ball has been "fielded" and thrown back to the wicket—or they are "out." A batsman is also "out" if a fielder catches the ball before it touches the ground. As noted, to make all the right decisions in judging the game, the umpire must be highly experienced, skilled, and fair.

Sports such as football, rugby, and cricket, once seen as men-only pursuits, now have parallel leagues of women's teams that are attracting ever larger audiences—thanks largely to increased TV coverage.

The Horse World
The horse world is big business. The Pony Club, the international youth organization, has some 50,000 members in the UK. Their competitive arenas are the local and national gymkhanas, which test the riding and jumping skills of the youngsters who compete. In addition, there are 36,000 members of the British Riding Club comprising 460 clubs across the UK. At the other end of the spectrum are the major professional horse-racing events that occur throughout the year.

The biggest event of the calendar is the annual Grand National, which takes place in April at Aintree, Liverpool. It is a punishing test of endurance for

young horses and their riders, both often totally unknown, and which attracts a "one-off" bet on the winner by vast numbers of the population who otherwise would never be seen in a betting shop. The race takes place over a 2.25-mile (3,600-meter) circuit (run twice) comprising thirty fences.

Marathon

There are other important participatory sports enjoyed in England, such as hockey and basketball, but it is marathon walking, especially the grueling 26.2-mile London Marathon, which has become an annual national event—a perfect vehicle for the English idiosyncratic collective character. (There is also the Newcastle-upon-Tyne Half Marathon). It is done in the name of charity—the British always like to support a good cause—and allows vast numbers of ordinary people to contribute, to achieve something (checking one's time is important and hoping to do better next year), and to have fun—some by just walking in outrageous costumes.

Golf

Of all the "leisure" sports, other than walking—which is a traditional pastime, well organized throughout the country by the Ramblers Association, which ensures that the public has access to the widest possible number of countryside walks—golf attracts the greatest number of participants. For many enthusiasts it has almost become a way of life. In 2011 there were some 1.3 million members of nearly 3,000 golf clubs that welcomed visiting golfers—and no self-respecting developer in Spain or Portugal would dream of investing in a resort aimed at British vacationers without including at least one golf course in his plans.

THE SEASON

In times gone by, the English "Season," as it is
known, was the preserve of the upper classes, who
would attend the top sporting and cultural events.
These, and private balls and parties, presented an
opportunity for showing off their eligible sons and
(particularly) daughters, chiefly in order to find
them suitable spouses, as well as showing themselves
and keeping up to date with the latest gossip. This
is still the case, of course, but socially speaking its
relevance is diluted as "new money" mixes with old.
Today the Season owes its survival to the members
of "corporate Britain," who use the main events as
sales and marketing opportunities.

Main Events

Other key sporting events of the year include the
Boat Race between Oxford and Cambridge on the
Thames (March); the Horse Trials at Badminton
(May); Derby Day at Epsom (June); racing at Royal
Ascot (July); tennis at Wimbledon (June–July);
rowing at Henley (July), and sailing at Cowes, on
the Isle of Wight (August).

Top cultural events include the Chelsea Flower Show (May); the Royal Academy's Summer Exhibition (June); and the opera at Glyndebourne in Sussex (May–September). The last night of the Promenade Concerts, held at the Albert Hall, London, each year, otherwise known as the "Proms," is also considered part of the fun, because it presents an entirely laudable opportunity for displaying good-natured patriotism by waving the Union Jack (Flag) and singing "Land of Hope and Glory" with great gusto at the end of the proceedings.

Naturally, if you go to any or all of these events you gain points for wearing the most fashionable clothes; you would consequently never go alone, but always with a group of friends or family, and would expect to see and be seen by a great many other friends and acquaintances.

PUBLIC HOLIDAYS
New Year's Day (January 1)
Good Friday (two days before Easter)
Easter Monday (the day after Easter)
Early Spring Holiday (first Monday in May)
Spring Holiday (last Monday in May)
Late Summer Holiday (last Monday in August)
Christmas Day (December 25)
Boxing Day (December 26)

DIY AND GARDENING

The weekend is the time when DIY ("Do It Yourself") and gardening enthusiasts change into their alter egos of craftsmen and begin or continue the process of transforming their homes and gardens. This is an extension of the concept that an "Englishman's home is his castle," and is a wonderful manifestation of an individual's sense of identity and singularity, as well as a source of self-satisfaction and achievement. Given the fact that home ownership in Britain—in England approximately 65 percent, although on the decline as renting is the only option for increasing numbers of younger workers—is the highest in Europe, it is not difficult to understand why the DIY retail sector always prospers when the economy prospers. The sector is led by nationwide chains of hardware supermarkets, and is given a further boost by TV makeover programs.

The quintessentially English pastime of gardening is enjoyed by men and women, young and old, through all the seasons. A garden epitomizes the English nostalgia for the country way of life, and for Blake's "green and pleasant land." The annual amount of money spent on garden-related products throughout the country is considerably greater than that spent on DIY. Gardening books, magazines, and programs on radio and TV are a major part of Britain's culture. The BBC's *Gardeners' Question Time* is the longest-running program of its kind, with its origins dating back to the mid-1940s.

Britain is full of wonderful stately homes, parks, and gardens, in both public and private ownership, that are open to visitors. Likewise, the National Gardens Scheme opens thousands of gardens in England and Wales to the public on certain days in the year in order to raise money for nursing and caring charities.

TRAVEL AND TRANSPORTATION

If you are driving, remember that in Britain you drive on the left. Roads are generally good (although economic hardship, post the world financial crisis, has affected road maintenance budgets), with a network of motorways (expressways), designated by an M, for example M1, M2, and so on, and lesser A and B roads, which are usually the more scenic routes for those who wish to see some countryside. Some rural roads are little more than winding tracks. The national speed limits are 70 mph (113 kmph) on motorways, 60 mph (97 kmph) on open roads, 40 mph (64 kmph) on dual carriageways (often on the outskirts of towns), and 30 mph (48 kmph) within towns (in some cases 20 mph, or 32 kmph). Be careful to watch your speeds.

Britain has a reasonable public transportation system. Everybody complains about it, but most forms of transportation generally run as scheduled. Trains are the fastest, of course, but the cheapest form of long-distance travel is by bus (coach). Nationwide scheduled coach services are run by National Express, and there are many other bus services operating around the country.

Britain's first (domestic) high-speed railway (known as HS1) runs at speeds of up to 140 mph (225 kph) on the 67-mile link from the Channel Tunnel at Folkestone to central London (St. Pancras). It uses the railway built for the Eurostar high-speed service to Paris and Brussels. A second, highly controversial, domestic high-speed railway (HS2) is planned to run from Euston (a short walk from St. Pancras) to Birmingham.

Britain has also been returning to traditional tramway systems in major cities, most recently in Nottingham and Edinburgh. In addition, Europe's biggest tunneling project, known as Crossrail, running east–west across London over a distance of 73 miles (26 miles of which involve tunnels), is due to open in 2018 and will include a link to Heathrow.

When traveling around Britain, it is a good idea to go to the local tourist information offices. They can help with accommodation, travel advice, and suggestions for what to see and do in the area.

chapter seven

FRIENDSHIP, FAMILY, & SOCIAL LIFE

INFORMALITY AND FRIENDSHIP

A view long held by many foreigners is that it takes time to make friends with the English (if at all), but that (occasionally) it can become something significant and permanent. Visitors continue to make this point and thus we have to accept that it is probably still true. On the other hand, the younger generations, who are more widely traveled, may well be far less reserved and "connect" much more readily. Even so, today's drive for cheerful informality, with the common use of first names in many areas of everyday life, especially the world of work, may give a different impression. It is based on the assumption that such informality makes everyone feel more comfortable and relaxed—but it does not necessarily equate with friendship and the desire to spend more time together outside the working environment or beyond a chance encounter in a holiday context. The best advice is not to push or assume too much.

This same principle holds true of neighbors ("the higher the fence, the better the neighbor"). On other occasions when people are brought together, for whatever reasons, such as when supporting local volunteer organizations, the English "reserve" tends to be very noticeable. People are happy to give up their time but not their privacy. Sometimes, this is seen as cold, or as bad manners; but it is probably simply politeness.

Understanding "Politeness"

The English form of politeness is sometimes misunderstood. Being polite in a formal context, such as in an office, may involve joining in and appearing to have a good time at a big social event organized by your company, or at a private dinner arranged by one of the directors. This is considered good manners; but for many English people, that's all it is. Likewise, if two strangers strike up a friendly conversation on a mainline train, for example, this is usually purely good manners, and the relationship is unlikely to develop further. In this context it should be noted that the "eleventh commandment" is that you should never attempt a conversation with a stranger while traveling on the London Tube (underground trains).

Greeting, Kissing, and Touching

The usual formal greeting is a "How do you do?" (or, less formally, "Hello") and a firm handshake, but with a lighter touch between men and women. A limp handshake from a man is considered insincere, effeminate, untrustworthy, or sloppy, or all four. Increasingly, the greeting "How are you?" is used, which is awkward because in principle it requires a reply that is best avoided. Instead the person greeted in this manner might respond by saying "Fine, thank you. Good to see you" or some similar response. It does not require a "How are you?" back.

On social occasions, say at a dinner party involving colleagues and their partners, handshakes between men and women give way to "social kissing," whereby the man lightly holds the woman by the upper arms and barely kisses the woman's cheeks, while the woman "kisses the air," making a soft (pretend kissing) "mmuh" sound. Increasingly, both cheeks are kissed. Close friends would exchange hugs and contact kisses.

Although, historically, the English are quite restrained and reserved, dislike exhibitionism in their day-to-day contact with others, and abhor "space invaders"—those who move too close during a conversation—hugging is now more prevalent, not least among the younger generation.

Within the family today, men play an increasing part in the traditional "mothering" role. The old situation of physical contact between father and son being restricted to a handshake—a formal standard of behavior that is still expected in a few "high society" contexts—has largely given way to a warmer physical relationship, although it should be added that in this context there continue to be significant regional differences.

MANNERS—FORMAL AND INFORMAL
Many British people admire the widespread use of the term "Sir" as a mark of respect in America, both inside and outside the classroom, including the home. In Britain the use of the term has largely disappeared in ordinary everyday life. It continues in schools—especially in public schools, where it is perceived as an essential courtesy in a more respectful and disciplined environment—and, of course, in the Armed Services.

Today young people in Britain show less deference to their elders, are generally much more relaxed about relationships, and take a more egalitarian, "laidback" view of society as a whole, and their place within it.

Terms of Endearment

The visitor to Britain is sometimes astonished to be addressed in rather intimate terms. In southern England, on the buses and in the shops, you may very well be addressed as "love," "lovey," "dear," "darling," "pet," or "petal"—and perhaps, if you are lucky, "my lover" in Devon. As you go north you will hear different terms, such as "chuck" (around Liverpool and the northwest), "duck" (around Sheffield and the northwest), and "hen" (in Scotland). As a market trader weighs up some apples for you, he might say, "Just over a kilo. All right, darlin'?" Don't be alarmed! These are all gentle terms of address, never intended to be overfamiliar or to offend. However, the tsunami of "political correctness" now overtaking historical regional idiosyncrasies in Britain may well put an end to such endearments in future years. It is certainly the case that some modern working women in metropolitan Britain view such old-fashioned terms of endearment as both patronizing and insulting.

"Thank You" and "Sorry!"

The British are strong on polite language. You will hear "Please," "Thank you," and "Sorry!" everywhere. Any service, however small, requires a "Thank you"—whatever you have just bought or paid for, whether it is a bus ticket, a trolleyful of groceries at the supermarket, a tankful of gas, or even a charity sticker when you have put some money in a donation box. And that is the end of it; the other person does not reply, as in the USA, "You're welcome," though they may say "Thank you" back, as a way of finishing off the conversation. The British say, "Thank you" when somebody pays them a compliment of any kind, they say, "Thank you, how kind of you" or simply "That's very kind of you" when somebody helps them with something. People on the radio or TV say, "Thank you" to the interviewer, presumably for the opportunity to give their opinion. The British are indeed a grateful lot!

Likewise, the word "Sorry" is also widely used among the British. Is this an example of British ultra-politeness, or just plain good manners? The British say, "Sorry!" almost involuntarily as an apology for any possible inconvenience or interruption for which he or she might feel responsible. They say, "Sorry!" or even "So sorry!" if they brush past somebody in the street, or touch somebody accidentally—invading somebody's private space. They may even say "Sorry" if somebody else treads on their toe (because their toe got in the way)! They say, "Sorry?" to signal the fact that they have not heard what someone has said, and to request repetition. ("Excuse me" is not normally used in any of these contexts, as it is in the United Stares—it is used to attract someone's attention, or in politely, or sometimes less politely, asking the person addressed to move aside.)

They will say, "I'm very sorry," or "I'm so sorry," as a sympathetic lead-in when giving some bad news, or when causing inconvenience or discomfort, such as when a doctor has to make a painful investigation. Even a traffic warden, when sticking a traffic violation notice on your car, may say, "Sorry, I'm only doing my job."

THE NEW FAMILIARITY

On Fridays, as one leaves work, it is a common courtesy to say to one's colleagues, "Have a good weekend." Another expression, "Have a nice day," learned from America, or the English version, "Have a good day," is now heard more often, not just from friends and colleagues, but from those at supermarket checkouts, and serving in shops and restaurants. This has been adopted as part of the informal friendliness of modern youth culture, along with another trend—the frequent use of customers' first names in day-to-day business dealings. Such familiarity is new to the traditionally reserved English, and often mildly irritates the older generations, who feel that such manners are presumptuous.

For the visitor, it is better to play safe and not address elderly people by their first names, unless invited to do so!

THE FAMILY
Children

The Victorian saying, "Children should be seen and not heard," may be seen as a contentious notion today, but is perhaps making a comeback. The feeling is simply that children should be reasonably well-behaved, and should not annoy other people by being excessively noisy or running around in an unruly way. While the quality of parenting in this context has varied considerably, the new generation of parents seems to understand the

need for order, structure, and discipline in day-to-day family life.

Thanks to the new technologies, media support, and a more enlightened view by educationalists, British children are encouraged to speak their mind at a much earlier age, and tend to be much more articulate than previous generations. They may be spending hours each day on their computers playing games or researching for their homework, but today's youngsters are generally better informed and more engaged than their parents were at the same age, and are encouraged to think about topical issues.

Many British children today live in a world of designer clothes, smart phones, tablets, gaming devices, partying, and media that address their every need (and whenever possible create new "needs"). Like their counterparts throughout the industrialized world, they have more disposable income ("pocket money") than ever before. Their preoccupation with social media, and their perception of self and sense of identity within them, has transformed the environment of family life and conventional social interaction.

The social protocols linked to the use of the new technology are in their infancy and largely incoherent. Couples can be seen in restaurants involved with their smart phones but not each other; levels of communication in families are subject to the preoccupations of children on their devices. It is a social revolution that has wide and as yet undocumented consequences.

At sixteen children can go into pubs on their own (and be served nonalcoholic drinks); they can legally have sexual intercourse, and marry with permission. At seventeen they can hold a driver's license, and at eighteen they can vote, purchase alcohol and tobacco, and join the Armed Services.

Family Meals
It is often regretted that today families rarely sit and eat meals together in the traditional way. It seems to be the case that in many families this is now limited to Sunday lunch or supper. With both parents working and children participating in after-school activities such as music lessons, or drama or sports clubs, meals in the working week tend to be *ad hoc*, to suit the various comings and goings. The evening meal will often be something quick and easy—such as a dish bought ready-made and heated in a microwave oven, pasta, "something out of a can," or a pizza delivered to the door—eaten not at a table but more likely on a sofa while watching TV or linked up to their electronic devices.

Visitors will notice that a significant number of permanent relationships these days (including younger family units) involve unmarried couples who refer to each other as their "partner" rather than their husband or wife.

Nannies

The children of the old aristocratic and upper-class families always had a nanny in attendance—a woman living in her own quarters in the house, who had complete care of them. She would sometimes stay for the rest of her life, looking after successive generations of children, and being regarded with great affection by the family.

Special training colleges, known for their high standards, were set up for "nursery nurses"; those nannies left with good qualifications and could expect the best jobs, with excellent pay and living conditions.

Demand for nannies grew in the economic "boom" years of the 1990s, mostly in cases where both father and mother had busy and well-paid professional careers. Contemporary society has seen a resurgence in the requirement for nannies—partly prompted by the huge increase of the super-rich living in London and elsewhere. "Nannying," trained or untrained (famously "Norland Nannies" are regarded as the best trained and most highly qualified nannies), became quite a popular job for young women, and many went to work in other countries, becoming one of Britain's successful cultural exports.

Pets

The British preoccupation with pets is huge. According to the Pet Food Manufacturers' Association, in 2014 the pet population of Britain amounted to 65 million—including fish—involving 13 million households (just under half). Of these, the largest group (24 percent) kept dogs as pets (9 million), followed by cats (8 million).

If there is a dog in a house that you are visiting, be aware that it may well be a situation of "love me, love my dog." In this case, the owner thinks the world of the dog, and does not believe that any sensible person could think otherwise—even though you might find it intensely intrusive, annoying, or even smelly!

Unfortunately many people underestimate the amount of time, money, and energy needed to look after pets, particularly, dogs. Every year before Christmas, there is a plea from animal care institutions and charities, such as the RSPCA (Royal Society for the Prevention of Cruelty to Animals), to think very carefully about buying a pet as a present. "A dog is not just for Christmas; it is for life" is the message. But thousands of unwanted dogs end up on the streets and in temporary care homes like the Battersea Dogs' Home in London.

The media frequently feature sentimental animal stories, for example about abandoned donkeys in a European country; and low-budget TV programs show pets doing "clever" or "amusing" things. Pet lovers also make the headlines from time to time when they leave their entire estate to a home for abandoned dogs or cats. In September 2014 a kennels in Manchester, housing some 150 dogs, caught fire, prompting dozens of people to drive (in some cases) considerable distances to offer their help and support, including rehousing the dogs that had survived.

The "animal rights" movement has had considerable impact on government policy; for example, research on live animals is now banned in the cosmetics industry, but is allowed under strict rules for scientific research for the benefit of human welfare.

Pet Travel Scheme
The Pet Travel Scheme, launched by the British government in 2000, allows pet cats and dogs from twenty-four Western European countries, and twenty-six "long-haul" countries, including Australia, New Zealand, Singapore, and Japan, to enter or reenter the UK without quarantine, provided they meet certain conditions, including vaccination against rabies.

Gift Giving
As suggested earlier, when visiting someone's home for a meal it is customary to bring flowers, chocolates, or a bottle of wine. Visitors coming to stay from overseas would do well to bring a gift for the parents and, perhaps, appropriate little presents typical of their own hometown or region for the children.

Gift giving in a more general sense, as for example in bringing presents for friends and family from exotic lands, is commonplace. Christmas (for most British people—not only the Christians) and birthdays are occasions for presents and parties. Younger people tend to be very spontaneous in gift giving and, among friends, tend to exchange presents and cards for birthdays and other occasions much more readily than their parents do. Mothering Sunday (Mother's Day) in March and Father's Day in June have become major annual landmarks for families: it is unthinkable that a child would not wish to send a card to each parent, often accompanied by flowers for Mothering Sunday.

THE CLASS SYSTEM

The following description is very generalized, and barely begins to cover all the many details and nuances of that very English phenomenon, "class." It is true to say, however, that the most telling indicators of an English person's class are his or her accent and behavior—in this matter the English can generally sum each other up within moments of meeting. In recent years, the BBC has endeavored to "normalize" regional accents through using news presenters and others from the regions. Thus, some would argue that the younger you are the less these "differences" matter, and in practice class is no longer a barrier to either casual social mixing or genuine friendship; but people often feel more comfortable associating with others from the same background. A working-class person might feel uncomfortable at a "society" wedding, for example, as might an aristocrat in a certain kind of pub, but this is a generalization, and in the modern world would bother fewer and fewer people; in any event, a certain amount of self-confidence would carry the day for both.

The Upper Class

The upper class generally refers to the aristocracy and its offshoots, and was traditionally the "ruling class," although this is no longer absolutely the case in today's fluid social mix. It largely consists of people with inherited wealth, and includes some of the oldest families in the land, many of

them titled. Along with land, wealth, titles, and privileges came certain obligations and responsibilities; not the least of these was the duty to behave as befitted one's rank. This is still the case among those who are genuinely "upper class"—good manners are of the utmost importance.

The upper class generally manages to keep itself to itself, minding its own business at all times. Many marriages continue to be "arranged" by a process of carefully managed introductions. Those who find themselves short of cash open their houses (the "stately homes of England," as they were famously put into song by Noël Coward) to the public and charge a fee for entry, or live in impoverished circumstances among some remaining priceless antiques.

Members of the upper class often have a distinctive, mannered accent, which is delivered in a very precise manner. A more slowly delivered version of this is known as "an upper-class drawl." Increasingly, however, the younger generation is inclined to avoid such mannerisms of speech in order *not* to appear upper class!

The upper class is defined first and foremost by the families that belong to it. To be from one of the "old" families is virtually a prerequisite of being upper class.

Other pointers are education (at good private schools such as Eton or Harrow, followed by university—Oxford or Cambridge); wealth (often, these days, in the form of land or property rather than cash); and, to a certain extent, occupation and pastimes, which include the traditional country sports of hunting, shooting, and fishing. Many upper-class people keep horses, and ride for pleasure and competitively (including show jumping), as well as taking an interest in racing.

Fox-Hunting

Over a hundred years ago, the playwright and satirist Oscar Wilde described fox-hunting as "the unspeakable in pursuit of the uneatable." Today, it has become a social and political battleground.

Those who opposed the sport did so on the grounds of cruelty to animals, and it became a major issue in Parliament until the Hunting Act of 2004 banned all hunting of wild animals with dogs in England and Wales. (Scotland had passed its own legislation two years earlier.) In other words, it was not so much a campaign to save the fox as a trophy in the battle between "rich" and "poor." It remains a contentious issue.

Those who are interested to know "who's who" in the aristocracy can consult *Burke's Peerage*, which gives the pedigrees of titled families. The principal "voice" of the upper class, however, is *The Tatler*—a weekly magazine that has been reporting on the rich and powerful for three hundred years. A recent BBC documentary went "inside" the periodical's offices to explore how it decides what to publish, especially how it manages to keep a balance between "old money" and "new money" (not least the impact of the considerable number of super-rich Russians now living in London), as well as contemporary values and expectations. Another important upper-class publication is *The Field*, which focuses on country life and sports.

The Middle Class
There has always been a middle class of those whose wealth or occupations put them somewhere between the aristocracy and the peasants and laborers. Landowners and professional people—"gentlemen"— were later joined by those who made money during or after the Industrial Revolution. The middle class is broadly based, and even divides itself into lower-middle and upper-middle, according to wealth, level of education, and perceived standing within the community. This refinement could be invented only by a society preoccupied with status, tribe, and the pursuit of difference.

The middle class these days encompasses the professional, managerial, and so-called "upwardly mobile" sections of society (as well, perhaps, as a "downwardly mobile" section from the upper class), and is seen to represent the greater part of the population as a whole, certainly in the southern half of England. It is generally less rigid in its behavior and in matters of etiquette than the upper class.

Middle-class values formed the backbone of society and provided the skilled professionals and administrators who ran the Empire. Education is important for the middle classes, at a private or good state school, preferably followed by university. Pastimes are not so well defined, but sports that call for expensive equipment, special clothing, or extensive training and practice, such as golf, tennis, and horse-riding, are regarded as a middle-class preserve.

Although they tend to approach life in a more relaxed way, like the upper class, the middle classes also enjoy establishment pomp and circumstance, such as the State Opening of Parliament by the Queen, the Garden Parties hosted by her at Buckingham Palace, or the pageantry associated with royal occasions, such as weddings and jubilees. Formal social occasions, such as a wedding or a ball for a daughter who is "coming out," that is, making her formal debut in society, are held in great style. Once an upper-class tradition, launching one's daughter in society in this way, in the hope that she will find a suitable husband, has now been taken up by the "new rich." The custom is encouraged by such publications as *The Tatler*, which features these debutantes and their parties in its pages.

The Working Class

"Working-class Britain" is a phrase still used by socialists and trade unionists. It was coined in the context of the exploitation and social inequality that resulted from the rise of nineteenth-century capitalism. Its use today continues to reinforce the historic class divisions of Britain, and of England in particular. On the other hand, in an attempt to remove what might have

been seen as a stigma and to be inclusive the main political parties today refer to "working people" and "hard working people"—meaning the entire working population.

Labour governments are always reminded that the Labour Party was founded by the trade union movement at the beginning of the twentieth century to champion the needs of its members. For most of its life the Party has been bankrolled through the trade union levy on its members.

The working class has its own rituals and etiquette that inform behavior and determine what is expected of its members. Working-class culture is projected and played out every week through the TV "soaps," principally *Coronation Street* (the longest-running), which reflects the way of life in the northeast of England, and *Eastenders*, which reflects life in and around London's East End. These soaps (and others, including *Emmerdale*, *Doctors*, and *Hollyoaks*, as well as *Neighbours* from Australia), of course, attract viewers from across the cultural spectrum.

Like the soaps, working-class life has traditionally revolved around the local pub, working men's clubs (women were, traditionally, never admitted, but political correctness has forced changes in recent times), soccer (known as football)—with at times almost tribal loyalty—betting shops, bingo halls, and brass bands, especially in the north. In its own way, it is a culture that also breeds its own form of snobbishness, which would quickly find fault with anyone who was thought to be stepping out of line, such as showing aspirations to rise "above his station," or class.

For example, there could be consequences within the community if somebody were to be seen joining the local fox hunt (which is considered upper class) or a smart local health club (which is seen as middle class) or supporting Rugby Union (which is seen as middle class) instead of Rugby League (which is seen as working class).

"Knowing One's Place"

A comic TV sketch of the 1970s perfectly sums up English attitudes to class. It features three men of different heights, dress, and headgear, standing in a row. The tallest and best-dressed of the three glances at the other two and says, "I look down on both of them." The man in the middle, dressed in an ordinary suit, turns to the tall man and says, "I look up to him"; then to the small man, dressed in working clothes with a cloth cap, and says, "but I look down on him." Finally, the smallest man just says, "I know my place." This sketch may seem an anachronism today, and in many respects it probably is, but the fact remains that class divisions continue to be recognized, even if not widely discussed other than by leaders of the traditional trade unions.

The "Chattering Classes"

There is a new cross-section of society, drawn from all classes, known as the "Chattering Classes." It consists of people involved in the media, whose business it is to tell the rest of the country what to think and why—from writers and journalists in the printed media, to those on TV and radio, and now the blogosphere and vlogsphere, together with academics, actors (increasingly these days), and those who inhabit the world of the arts generally. Many of them are also politicians.

One of their characteristics is that they take themselves, and their mission of setting the social and cultural agenda, very seriously. As a group they tend to allow themselves to be ruder than other people, because of how they view their own importance.

But, like politicians, they live a life somewhat apart, and are usually greeted with a healthy skepticism by the rest of society. They are also the promoters of what is increasingly regarded as a modern social bugbear, "political correctness"—the proscribed barriers to the use of language or behavior that could be perceived as offensive to any one (minority) group. Thus, we now have "chairperson," or even "chair," instead of the generic "chairman," or "firefighters" rather than "firemen."

The chattering classes give lively parties, and are stimulating company.

The "*Nouveaux Riches*"

This is a disparaging term, but the class is as old as history. It specifically refers to those who make an ostentations display of newly acquired wealth. It can include the self-made man, who from humble beginnings has accumulated a great deal of money, probably from trade, or the suddenly rich millionaire, such as a lottery winner. Such a person might for example buy an unnecessarily large and luxurious house or car—which is seen as vulgar or tasteless— or start throwing huge and extravagant parties.

In today's social environment many of the traditional self-made people, whether industrialists or tradesmen, also tend to receive a public "honour" as well. Those modest people who do not make a great display of their new wealth are treated with due respect and would not be described as "*nouveau riche*."

Read the Books!
The writer and lawyer John Mortimer, creator of *Rumpole of the Bailey* (originally shown on TV 1975–92)—a richly comic observation of English customs and moral attitudes as seen through the eyes of an old-fashioned barrister (advocate)—once remarked that the basis of all English literature is class—moving from Chaucer, through Shakespeare, through Trollope, to the present day. Read almost any piece of fiction by an English author, and it will give you further insight into the manners and mores of the English.

"Lifestyle," not "Class"
Finally, what is increasingly being called "lifestyle" could well be the next paradigm in the shifting notions of class. Driven by "Yuppies" ("young, upwardly mobile professional people") and "Dinks" (couples with "dual income, no kids"), and reinforced by a growing media fixation on youth culture and the cult of celebrity, the lifestyle gurus preach a gospel of instant access and "must have now" to a quality of life determined not by wealth, education, moral values, or merit, but by the fashion of the moment—the color you paint your bedroom, the positioning of your furniture (*feng shui*), and the designer clothes you wear. The followers of "lifestyle" may well see themselves as the new social leaders!

TABOO SUBJECTS
In the context of polite conversation, the traditional social taboos used to be politics, sex, and religion. To this might be added the subject of money. These

subjects were all considered likely to raise tempers or cause embarrassment, and thus disturb the atmosphere at the dinner table. Today some things have changed, but vestiges of the old feelings persist, and visitors should be careful before saying anything that might cause offense or embarrassment. Religion is not a subject for discussion if you are unsure of your company.

Money
The subject of money—in the sense of how much or how little one has—is not for general discussion, being thought too personal and a rather vulgar thing to talk about. Also, even in today's world of the National Lottery and the TV game show *Who Wants to be a Millionaire?*, there are still some English people who think that there is something rather disreputable about being "in trade." In other words, the perception of money-making being somewhat tainted lingers.

On the other hand, it is perfectly acceptable to talk about how you have managed to save in small ways—such as finding a bottle of good wine for half price in a supermarket!

The British upper classes are deeply suspicious of conspicuous consumption, or "showing off"; but this generalization is often stood on its head by the increasing numbers of newly rich (not least the estimated 100,000 Russians living in London), many of whom are very enthusiastic about displaying their wealth. In Britain demonstrable wealth is not necessarily the measure of success. People are admired because, as in sport, they took part— they had a go. Perhaps they failed; but they will be admired more for who they are (essentially as a person, although it may include status) and how they conduct their lives. It is a fact that someone from the upper classes who finds himself with no money and no prospects will usually be treated with more respect than a person with no manners or "breeding," who is in a similar situation. In the end, dignity, culture, and status are more highly regarded than the possession of money.

Politics is OK
With the arrival of the televising of Parliament, especially "Prime Minister's Question Time" on Wednesdays, the heated debates that took place before (and after) the referendum on Scottish independence in 2014, the arrival of the UK Independence Party as a new voice in British politics, numerous political scandals, the promotion of gay rights (including marriage), attitudes to the political processes in modern Britain have become much more polarized and vociferous. Despite low turnouts in local elections, and the general view that there is a serious disconnect between people and those who govern them, politics have become energized—attitudes are changing, and increasingly people are becoming more articulate in expressing their views socially and in the public arena.

Sex Is More OK Than It Was
The British seem to have had an odd relationship with sex for a long time, but these days they are far more relaxed about its place in contemporary society—a return perhaps to the less prudish times of earlier generations, perhaps as early as Chaucer's England! Thus, explicit sex scenes in TV dramas are now common, as is sex-related humor, and sex-related

articles in just about every periodical, from
magazines directed at youth to general-interest titles,
and the vast array of women's weekly or monthly
publications. Accordingly, some visitors may be
shocked. One's own sex life, however, is as private
as one wishes.

Attitudes toward sexuality have never been
straightforward historically. This ambivalence
has sometimes generated extreme outcomes—
from periods of repression, as in the Puritan
Commonwealth of Oliver Cromwell (1649–60),
or the reign of Queen Victoria (1837–1901), when
some people even covered piano legs out of perverse
notions of modesty, to periods of excess as in the
Regency period of the early nineteenth century, or
indeed, some might say, today.

Sex and sexual repression have been a major
preoccupation of British writers, dramatists, artists,
entertainers, and social reformers for generations—
the long-running farce in London's West End, *No
Sex, Please, We're British* (1971–87), is a classic
example of its genre. In the meantime, after the so-
called "sexual liberation" of post-1960s Britain, the

country has the third-highest divorce rate in the EU (mostly initiated by women) and the highest number of single mothers under the age of twenty. On the other hand, the divorce rate among the younger generation is dropping, whereas those over sixty—the "silver splitters" is up by nearly 50 percent in a decade. Both written and broadcast media support sexual freedom in terms of choice and orientation, and even preteen magazines promote interest in sex, directly and indirectly.

What Does the Foreign Visitor Do?
Of course, it is difficult for an outsider to know exactly who is who and what should be what in any particular social context in England. The better news, however, is that nothing is expected of a foreigner except to have good manners. A visitor who simply "fits in" is welcomed.

If a visitor from overseas has bad manners, this would not be mentioned, but would simply reinforce the traditional English view that social order and civility cease at the White Cliffs of Dover.

chapter eight

BUSINESS BRIEFING

BRITAIN'S ECONOMY

Until the international banking crisis triggered a world recession in 2009, the economy had been one of the success stories of the New Labour administration (1997–2010). Britain had maintained low inflation and the lowest interest rates in a generation, achieving annual growth of around 2.5 percent—against a backdrop of a boom in the service and knowledge-based sectors but a depressed manufacturing base—as

well as maintaining an independent currency. At the same time, the government levied the largest increases in indirect taxation in a generation to fund an increase in spending on public services, especially the National Health Service. After the elections of 2010, the Conservative–Lib Dem coalition introduced swingeing cuts to reduce the budget deficit.

At the time of writing, almost five years later (some months before the general election), the British economy had become the most successful in Europe, with a growth rate of 2.6 percent, supported by a continuing expansion of the service sector, yet faltering growth in the manufacturing sector.

However, in terms of scientific research, Britain has become a leading world player. Recent high-profile examples include the contribution of British scientists to the successful placing of the Rossetta space probe's lander onto a comet nucleus, in cancer research the first positive results in 2014 of new drugs that harness the body's immune system to attack cancer cells, and the treatment of a paralyzed man with a completely severed spinal chord, albeit made public in the early stages of recovery.

Britain's principal trading partner is the European Union (accounting for over 50 percent of trade in goods and services), with Germany the biggest trading partner (11.3 percent) both within and without the EU (which meant Germany displaced the US as the UK's principal trading partner, which stood at 10.5 percent, as of 2013). In the old days, of course, it had been the British Empire. In fact, the loss of Empire with its captive markets has forced British industry and commerce to become far more competitive. A "wake-up" call was first sounded by Margaret Thatcher in the 1980s, but only slowly and to some extent reluctantly has it been implemented. It is ironic that four of the ten most productive car plants in the whole of Europe are in Britain, but foreign owned— Honda, Toyota, Nissan, and Vauxhall Motors (GM).

Furthermore, Britian still manufactures many of the world's premium and sports marques, including Aston Martin, Bentley, Jaguar, Lotus, MG, and Rolls Royce, demonstrating that the British worker can indeed be one of the best, given the right working environment and motivation. The British work more hours than any other country in Europe, coming fourth in the world, after the USA, Japan, and Australia, in the total number of hours worked during the year.

Britain's biggest foreign investor is the United States, and vice versa. This is not surprising, since these countries have a common history, language, and culture. It is important, however, to recognize that there can be significant differences in the perception of history, in the use of language, and in cultural norms and aspirations. This is not the place to examine these issues in detail, but it is useful for American visitors, especially businessmen, to be aware of the fact that such differences do exist. Britain's share of Nobel Prizes is second only to that of the US in absolute terms, but is twice as many per capita.

As islanders, the British are a mercantile race by nature. Trading with the rest of world is a routine part of commercial and industrial daily life, as it has been since long before the days of Empire. In fact, although it has less than 1 percent of the world's population, Britain is the world's sixth-largest trading nation. This "overseas" trade, as it is called, today accounts for approximately 23 percent of GDP and continues to be a vital component of the national economy.

Britain's principal markets (total share of exports) are Germany (11.3 percent), the United States

(10.5 percent), the Netherlands (8.8 percent), France (7.4 percent), and the Irish Republic (6.2 percent). Conversely, the top five suppliers are almost the same, with Germany leading, followed by the US, China, the Netherlands, and Norway.

Traditional manufacturing industries, including the "heavy" industries of coal, iron, and steel, like those of the G7 group generally, continue to decline, with the service sector continuing to expand (led by financial services), currently accounting for 79 percent of GDP. In the manufacturing sector, aerospace leads the way, followed by automotive, pharmaceuticals, and North Sea oil and gas.

BUSINESS FORMALITIES
The Handshake

When you first meet businesspeople, and also on leaving, there will be the usual round of firm (but not bone-crunching, and not protracted) handshakes. Typical greetings are, "Hello; nice to meet you," or the traditional "How do you do?"(which does not require a reply). Increasingly, the latter greeting is being replaced by "How are you?" but does not require a "How are you?" back. In responding to a "thank you" for a service rendered, whatever the context, some British people have adopted the Australian reply of "No problem, or the American "You're welcome."

Business Cards

The handshake is generally, but not always, followed by the exchange of business cards. Cards for the professional classes, including civil servants, are usually discreet, simple designs with black ink on a white background. For those involved in, say, manufacturing, marketing, or public relations, they are more colorful and include the company logo. Unlike the Japanese, who study the contents of the card, especially the status of the giver, the British tend simply to glance at the card without studying it, pocket it, and reciprocate with one of their own, if they have one.

The Value of Good Manners

The British believe that manners "makyth man" and are especially good for business too. Quiet courtesy will make a very positive impression on your host. Show a degree of reticence and deference, and remember to say, "please," "thank you," and so on.

First Names

Take the lead from your host regarding the use of first names; as a general rule it is best to take things gradually. Age differences and status are also a determinant. As noted earlier, younger people (and the young at heart!) are more inclined to use first names, American-style, but you need to be sure of your ground before assuming this is the level of communication preferred by your host. It is a fact, too, of course, that the wide use of e-mail has had a significant impact on communications; the American protocol of "Hi Peter" is widespread, but English traditionalists often prefer the conventional letter-writing format, using "Dear Peter," or even "Hello Peter."

Friendship, and Being Friendly
Bear in mind that the British tend to compartmentalize their lives and have a heightened sense of privacy and personal space. This is reinforced by adherence to the old axiom of "never mix business and pleasure"—hence a reticence to "make friends" in business, in the sense of close relationships. People are often aware of the possibility of spoiling a good working relationship by making a presumption of something closer. For many of the younger generation this is no longer the barrier it once was. However, there is a world of difference between being friendly toward someone and assuming that this is real friendship.

WRITTEN COMMUNICATIONS
The forms of address that include the terms "Mr.," "Mrs.," "Miss," or "Ms." continue to be used, and are probably still considered the "normal" mode. However, in general correspondence the practice is growing of writing simply "John Smith," "Jane Smith," or even "J. Smith."

Recognition of an individual's professional status, such as Dr. (medical or academic doctor) or Professor, or rank within the Armed Services, etc., is the required etiquette. Very few people, however, particularly in private correspondence, continue to use the traditional form of address to a gentleman, "Esquire," as in "John Smith, Esq.," and the practice is very likely to disappear within a generation.

FORMAL MEETINGS AND DRESS CODE

The days of the rolled umbrella, dark suit, and bowler hat have practically disappeared—with the occasional exception in the City of London. On the other hand, regardless of some relaxation of dress codes in certain contexts (see below), smart dressing for business meetings is essential. This means suits for men, and a neat skirt or trousers and jacket for women. The tie is frequently absent today and has been replaced by, for example, colored striped or gingham shirts. "Color" in the workplace is much more evident. Personal hygiene and a well-groomed appearance are important. There is widespread use of fragrance these days for both men and women; subtlety is still your best friend in this department.

"Dressing Down"

In the 1990s and into the new century, various large and small companies acceded to the requests of staff to create a more relaxed atmosphere on Fridays, the end of the working week, by what has been called "dressing down," that is, by coming to work in smart but casual clothes, and not wearing a conventional shirt and tie. This concession most benefited the male workforce, given that women had for some time been wearing the kind of fashionable clothing that could hardly have been imagined a generation before.

Men's Lib

In 2003 a male worker in the back office (that is, not dealing with the public) of a government agency won a case of discrimination against his employer, who had insisted that he wear a suit and tie to work at all times.

Punctuality

Being on time for appointments is essential in a
business context. Don't be late. On the other hand,
don't arrive too early (other than a few minutes at
most). This rule also holds for evening arrangements,
for example where you are expected for dinner at a
restaurant. If you are unavoidably held up, telephone.

An exchange of pleasantries is expected at the start
of a meeting; but avoid excessive loudness, trying too
hard to be humorous, being over-familiar, or even
being excessively polite with those above you.

Business Lunches

With an eye on costs and the pressures of time,
extended business lunches are rare these days. If you
are invited to a business lunch (usually taken from
12:30 p.m. onward) you should assume that you will
be back in the office by around 2:30 p.m. Entertaining
clients in the evening is not particularly common,
except when there is an occasion such as a trade fair.

Increasingly, employees take a short lunch break,
sometimes going for a quick walk and bringing back
a sandwich to eat in the office.

SMOKING IN OFFICES/PUBLIC PLACES

Since 2007 Britain has been a smoke-free zone.
Smoking has been banned in all public indoor
spaces, especially on public transportation, and in
offices, theaters, cinemas, and restaurants. Office
workers desperate for a cigarette can be seen puffing
away outside on the sidewalk. Pub landlords had
raised concerns that the ban would have a negative
impact on sales. A few years on, the impact has been
mixed. Many pubs have indeed closed down, while

others have developed their food sales. The drop in the number of adult smokers (over eighteen) in Britain has been dramatic; current estimates are that 18.7 percent of the adult population in Britain smoke, with some 2.1 million smoking e-cigarettes. There remains a problem with sixteen-to-eighteen-year - olds, with some 20 percent still smoking, despite the government's vigorous anti-smoking campaigns.

GIFT GIVING

Exchanging lavish gifts is not usually expected or done in a British business context. The British are generally not at ease with this practice elsewhere in the world, and struggle with it when formalities require it at home. They are embarrassed if they receive a generous gift, and even more embarrassed if they have to give one. Whether this has to do with a perception that gifts contain an element of bribery, or is simply a manifestation of traditional English shyness and reticence, is debatable. It may also be that in a business relationship a gift seems too personal.

To help the process along, there has been a huge growth in the corporate gift market—"sanitized" gifts with the company logo on them, from umbrellas to ballpoint pens. But this is all done in the cause of good marketing and public relations. At product launch parties and similar events, it is increasingly common to be given a "goodie bag" on leaving containing a few "useful" items supposedly related to the business activity of the giver.

For the visitor bringing gifts, remember they will not necessarily be reciprocated. But don't let this deter you! A present of food or wine or craftwork from your country will always be welcomed.

BUSINESSPEOPLE

The hard realities of doing business in the twenty-first century leave little room for those who used to fine-tune class differences when it came to a choice of employees. Automatic access to the world of work via the "old school tie" has gone, although making useful contacts ("networking") is important. Survival in today's competitive environment has forced management everywhere to become tougher and employ people for their efficiency, multitasking capabilities, and capacity to contribute to the organization in a direct and positive way—not for their looks, social connections, or cultured voice. A new meritocracy has evolved, as well as greater transparency in the way companies operate.

Accountants now tend to be at the center of decision-making, and the considerable tightening of financial rules and regulations, including anti-discriminatory laws (notably sexual and racial discrimination), require increasing transparency in the way business is conducted and seen to be conducted.

At the start of 2014, according to the Federation of Small Businesses (FSB), there were an estimated 5.2 million businesses in the UK, employing some 25.2 million people. Of these, small and medium-sized companies (SMEs) accounted for some 99.3 percent of all British enterprises, responsible for 47.8 percent of private sector employment and 33 percent of private sector turnover. The FSB itself has some 200,000 members, whose businesses employ an average of seven people, including the owners. Not surprisingly, apart from many thousands of shopkeepers and café owners, among these there are many traditional and family firms—making a wide array of products from cheeses and wines to shirts and concert pianos.

These firms are part of the fast-disappearing "skilled craftsmen" foundations that have been at the heart of British entrepreneurial culture for a century and more. Even basic domestic tradesmen, such as plumbers, electricians, and carpenters are increasingly hard to find, partly because the old apprenticeship system was abandoned a generation ago (although the government has made some recent efforts to encourage a simpler version of it through its Skills Funding Agency for sixteen-to-twenty-four-year-olds), and partly because government attempts at social engineering within the school system have not encouraged trade-oriented syllabuses.

Women in Business

Equal rights for women in the world of work are enshrined in law; but there are areas where the "glass ceiling" continues to inhibit women's advancement and equal pay has yet to be achieved. Nevertheless, there are today more women at the top than ever before. Also, the government benefits system is more generous to women, particularly single and working mothers, than ever before.

Despite this, outside the office, such as at trade fairs, conferences, or seminars, many men are still inclined to assume that the women present are probably personal assistants or support staff, so as a woman you would do well to make your executive/managerial position clear at the earliest opportunity—obviously in as subtle and gracious a manner as possible.

NEGOTIATION STYLES

In Britain negotiation and interview styles are markedly different from those in the United States. The British business interview and negotiating

style tends to be deferential, indirect, affable, and relaxed, where humor is not necessarily out of place. The American style tends to be shorter and much more direct, where individuals sell themselves hard, leaving the other side in no doubt regarding their strengths and merits. Pleasantries are typically not exchanged.

Remember, too, in this context, that given the typical English inclination toward self-effacement and understatement, you may have to exercise great patience in doing business at this level. If it is generally true that Americans like to be "sold" something, it is equally true that the English generally like to "buy" something, and they can sometimes take an inordinate amount of time to make up their minds. So do not expect a hard sell in Britain. Everything will be understated, and you may well have to probe and even pester in order to determine the real value of the product or service that interests you. In other words, you will actually need to ask!

TRADE UNIONISM

The reform of trade unionism in the Thatcher years helped to bring about the rebirth of the British economy in the mid 1980s. The prosperity that followed has continued more or less uninterrupted ever since—apart from two major storms the economy had to contend with. First was Britain's sudden withdrawal in 1991 from the European Monetary Union (EMU), which caused huge increases in interest rates, resulting in many people losing their homes, and businesses going bust. The second was the fallout from the world financial crisis of 2007–8 followed by the tax and spending policies of the Labour government, which prompted the austerity measures of the incoming coalition government of 2010. These experiences have triggered a revival of trade union activism and a hardening of left of center positions, resulting in a return to public sector strike action, including teachers, police, hospital support staff, the fire and rescue service, and all elements of transportation, including the London Tube and bus services.

VACATIONS

The average national vacation entitlement is approximately twenty working days (this excludes teachers, who get more), plus the standard public holidays (see Chapter 6). It is accepted that the typical summer vacation will be a maximum of two consecutive weeks, unless a longer period, if available to the employee, has been arranged with the employer beforehand.

The Christmas and New Year period now also tends to extend to two consecutive weeks (outsiders

have accused Britain of "closing down" at this time).
Many companies now insist that this end-of-year
vacation is mandatory, and forms part of the annual
holiday entitlement (apart from Christmas Day,
Boxing Day, and New Year's Day, which are official
public holidays). Covering for absent clerical and
administrative colleagues is increasingly required in
employment contracts—an exception, perhaps,
being the Civil Service.

CONCLUSION
These pages have explored many aspects of the
so-called "British" character and what it is to be
"British"; but as we have seen, this belies the real
truth that it is in its diversity that the "Great"
in "Great Britain" really belongs, never mind its
political significance. It is this rich variety that makes
Britain what it is today. Extraordinarily, despite
the diversity, there exist an overarching feeling of
belonging and a sense of common values that give
the country its unique character. On the other
hand, some might argue that following the Scottish
Independence Referendum in 2014, fissure lines in
the body politic have begun to appear and notions
of a nationalist revival in England itself have begun
to be articulated across society, epitomized in the
slogan "English votes for English laws." In this
context, it is important to understand that in
modern times, Britain has never had to manage
so much change—socially, economically, and
politically—in so short a time.
    Yet, it is out of this historical and cultural jigsaw
that the British "genius" has evolved: a genius for
survival as well as creativity. Against the odds, the

monarchy in recent years is more popular than ever, the BBC remains the world's most respected public broadcaster, the people's capacity for fair-mindedness, tolerance, and compromise (although severely tested) is as strong as ever, and the country is still producing highly gifted individuals capable of sending a sophisticated robotic space probe (in conjunction with the European Space Agency) to land on a comet, or create a regeneration solution for an injured spine through the application of cultivated cells from a patient's nose.

The British continue to be stubborn but courteous, funny but infuriating, friendly but slow to make friends. Britain remains a remarkable and fascinating conundrum—to itself as well as to the outside world.

Further Reading

There is a vast range of books on every conceivable aspect of Britain. Here are a few titles to start with.

Andrews, Robert, et al. *Rough Guide to England*. Rough Guides Ltd: London, 2015.

Bingham, Harry. *This Little Britain: How One Small Country Changed the Modern World*. London: HarperCollins, 2009.

Bryson, Bill. *Notes from a Small Island*. London: Transworld Publishers, 1995.

Davies, John. *A History of Wales*. London: Penguin Books, 2007.

—— *The Celts: Prehistory to Present Day*. London: Cassell, 2002.

DK Eyewitness Travel Guide: Great Britain. London: Dorling Kindersley, 2014.

Fox, Kate. *Watching the English: The Hidden Rules of English Behaviour*. Boston/London: Nicholas Brealey Publishing, revised and updated edition, 2014.

Jackson, Michael. *Malt Whisky Companion*. London: Dorling Kindersley, 6th edn., 2012.

Lyall, Sarah. *The Anglo Files: A Field Guide to the British*. New York: W. W. Norton, 2008.

Marr, Andrew. *A History of Modern Britain*. London: Pan Books, 2009.

Michelin Green Guide to Scotland. Watford, Herts: Michelin Travel Publications, 7th edn, 2013.

Michelin Green Guide to Great Britain. Watford, Herts: Michelin Travel Publications, 2012.

Morgan, Kenneth O. *Oxford History of Britain*. Oxford: University of Oxford Press, 2010.

Paxman, Jeremy. *The English: Portrait of a People*. London: Penguin Books, 1999.

Ross, David. *Scotland: History of a Nation*. Glasgow: Gresham Publishing, 2014.

——*England: History of a Nation*; *Wales: History of a Nation*.

Steves, Rick. *Great Britain*. Berkeley, California: Avalon Travel, 2014.

culture smart! britain

Index